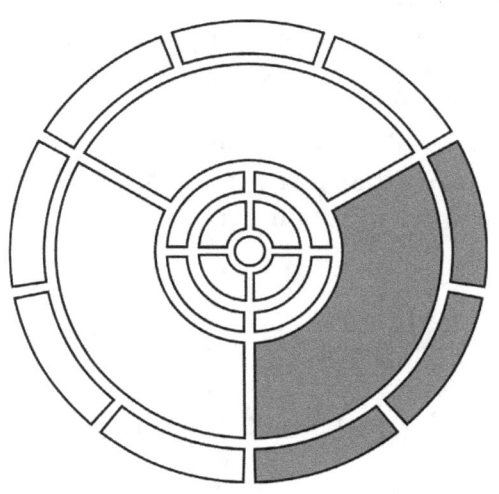

TEAMWORK & CULTURE

Brett Thomas

How the Most Successful Leaders Create the
Container, Communicate Effectively and Keep
Everyone Engaged and Motivated

First Print Edition, February 2025

Copyright © 2023-2025 Brett Thomas and Integral Publishing, LLC

No part of this publication may be reproduced, stored in a retrieval system, or transmitted in any form or by any means, electronic, mechanical, photocopying, recording, or otherwise, without written permission of the publisher.

ISBN 9798311403559

Published by Integral Publishing, LLC

First published November 2023
First print version February 2025

CONTENTS

INTRODUCTION 1

CHAPTER 1: WHY MOST LEADERSHIP DEVELOPMENT EFFORTS FAIL 5

CHAPTER 2: THE LEADERSHIP ROSETTA STONE 21

CHAPTER 3: THE UNIVERSAL LEADERSHIP MODEL 35

CHAPTER 4: THE ACCELERATING LEADERSHIP METHODOLOGY 53

CHAPTER 5: BENCHMARKING TEAMWORK & CULTURE LEADERSHIP CAPACITY 117

CHAPTER 6: CREATING THE CONTAINER 131

CHAPTER 7: COMMUNICATION 185

CHAPTER 8: MEANINGFUL MOTIVATION 245

CONCLUSION: WHERE TO GO FROM HERE ON YOUR LEADERSHIP JOURNEY 275

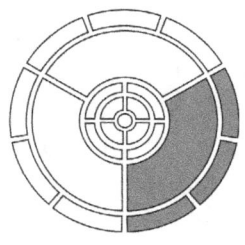

INTRODUCTION

This book introduces you to a major breakthrough in the field of leadership and leadership development. In a field where most so-called "experts" cannot even agree on a single definition of leadership, and the vast majority of leadership development programs fail, many of my clients and readers appreciate the clarity that this *Integral Leadership* book series brings to a confusing and often overwhelming topic. *Teamwork & Culture* is the next groundbreaking book on rapid leadership development in this series. This book provides detailed practices, techniques and leadership skills that help managers and executives set their people up for success, create and maintain a conducive environment, including a healthy culture and emotional climate, and keep people engaged and motivated using appropriate and effective communication, including feedback, listening, collaboration and conflict management.

Unlike most books on leadership that focus on abstract concepts and vague "leadership qualities," this book drills right down into specific, tangible techniques that amount to the exact behaviors that make leaders successful in this crucial dimension of leadership.

Many leaders face significant challenges when it comes to teamwork and culture. Low morale, disengaged employees, and communication breakdowns frequently undermine team effectiveness. Leaders often struggle to cultivate psychological safety, ensuring that team members feel comfortable taking risks, making mistakes, and voicing concerns without fear of repercussions. The complexity of managing a diverse workforce, including remote and hybrid teams, further compounds these challenges. Without a well-structured culture and communication framework, conflicts escalate, collaboration suffers, and motivation declines.

This essential addition to the Integral Leadership book series provides leaders with the techniques, tools, and leadership skills necessary to build high-performance teams, foster a thriving organizational culture, and keep employees engaged and motivated. Rather than relying on abstract theories about leadership qualities, this book focuses on specific, proven behaviors that enable leaders to create an environment where individuals and teams can excel.

This Integral Leadership handbook equips leaders with field-tested strategies to create a strong team foundation. Readers will learn how to design and sustain a high-trust culture, ensuring that people feel valued, included, and empowered. Communication techniques help leaders master active listening, constructive feedback, and conflict resolution, fostering open dialogue and collaboration. This book also explores intrinsic motivation—moving beyond outdated extrinsic incentives to unlock the deeper psychological drivers that sustain engagement and commitment.

This book offers a practical, results-driven approach to team leadership, making it an essential guide for managers, executives, and organizational leaders who are committed to creating a culture of trust, collaboration, and high performance.

It also presents a compelling argument as to why the "bogus" leadership development industry is not truly developing leaders. It introduces the world's first "Unifying Theory of Leadership" and reveals my 25 year "trade secret" on how we consistently achieve outstanding results with our leadership development programs (in an industry where that generally produces lackluster results).

The approach to leadership and leadership development outlined in this book is almost certainly unlike anything you've ever seen before. Most leadership trainings and many books about leadership fail to define the specific abilities, skill sets, techniques and behaviors that make up the complex skill called leadership. In fact, most so-called leadership experts don't even recognize that leadership is a complex skill.

This book is the remedy for that. The information contained within is based on my 25 years of experience advising leaders, training leaders, and coaching leaders and executive teams. This experience avails me a unique perspective about which methods actually produce improvements in leadership skills, as opposed to those that only increase a leader's knowledge of concepts but do little to change their behavior.

I am approaching this book as a conversation with you, the reader. I am assuming that in your role of leader, you already are familiar with many aspects of leadership (and leadership development). If you find this "conversation" valuable, I hope we can continue the conversation in my other books that unpack and expand upon the ideas introduced here. I expect that this will be one of the most valuable books you've ever read on leadership.

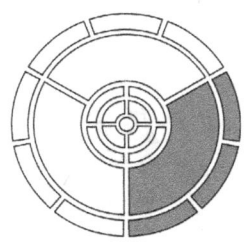

CHAPTER 1: WHY MOST LEADERSHIP DEVELOPMENT EFFORTS FAIL

Many studies from best-in-class organizations, institutions and publications in recent years have drawn the same conclusion: most leadership development efforts fail. This is no exaggeration, this is simply a matter of fact that is easily verified. Numerous studies from prominent institutions (including McKinsey and Harvard) estimate that approximately 80 cents of every dollar spent on leadership development is wasted. I have personally reviewed numerous studies that back up this assertion. This also tracks closely with my two-decades of experience training and coaching leaders, and also reviewing leadership development programs and interviewing facilitators and participants who have gone through typical leadership development programs. I have devoted my professional career to this field of leadership development and it has been of great interest to me to stay on top of the current industry practices and compare my unique methodology to what my peers and competitors are doing. I am very familiar with how leadership training and coaching is typically done (and how it is very slowly evolving).

Most leadership training programs amount to one and two week classroom seminars with lectures about leadership character traits, leader qualities, or abstract concepts that have little bearing on learning the actual concrete techniques (behaviors) that can improve leadership performance.

I'm sure you have come into contact with this problem. When you try to read books, attend leadership seminars or speak to executive coaches, it seems that they all have a different idea of what constitutes effective leadership, and their ideas largely contradict each other.

Bernard Bass, the well-respected leadership researcher and author of *The Bass Handbook of Leadership: Theory and Managerial Applications,* has noted, "Any two-day conference on leadership begins with one day of argumentation about what leadership means."

Many business professors, when speaking candidly, admit this fact that no one can agree on a definition or description of effective leadership. MIT Sloan management professor John Van Maanen has stated, "Even today, three-plus decades in, there's no real definition of it."

William Deresiewicz, the author of the book, *Excellent Sheep,* points out while every college in the country claims to be producing leaders, no one appears to know what the word even means. "There seem to be two possibilities," he writes, "The first is that it means nothing at all, or whatever definition is useful at any given time. The second is that it simply means being in charge."

Another well-known theorist, Fred Fiedler, observed, "There are almost as many definitions of leadership as there are leadership theories—and there are almost as many theories of leadership as there are psychologists working in the field."

The reason why there is almost no agreement among leadership advice givers on a single definition of "effective leadership" is that each different "type" of follower and leadership advice giver looks for different qualities and behaviors in what they consider to be "effective leaders".

This is because all followers and all advice-givers have one of our different worldviews. I will introduce these worldviews as a central part of my model in later chapters.

Here, I will mention that leadership advice is often bogus because instead of *one* definition of effective leadership, there are actually *four* definitions. Each of the four camps of advice givers has its own definition of effective leadership, which essentially amounts to them using their definition of "effective leadership" to push their own unconscious bias. The field of leadership theory and leadership development is riddled with unconscious bias and represents one of the biggest reasons so much of it is so bogus.

Few, if any, contextualize their definition of effective leadership by saying, this is a definition of effective leadership for "traditional types" or for "postmodern" or "progressive" types. Rather, they just push their unconscious bias and suggest their definition of effective leadership (for one of the worldviews) as the most effective way to lead all four types of followers. This is, of course, untrue, but that doesn't stop them from saying it.

It is no exaggeration to say that the advice givers in the leadership industry have failed to provide a definition or description of effective leadership that they can agree to.

Barbara Kellerman, a Harvard professor, takes it one step further when she says the leadership industry has failed. She explains, "The leadership industry has failed over its roughly 40 year history to improve the human condition in any major, meaningful, measurable way."

She is one of the few honest leadership professors who doesn't pull punches. Kellerman is a distinguished professor at Harvard University's John F. Kennedy School of Government. She was the Founding Executive Director at Harvard's Kennedy School's Center for Public Leadership, and previously served as the Director of the Center for the Advanced Study of Leadership at the Academy of Leadership at the University of Maryland. Kellerman has written a series of books that amount to scathing take downs of the bogus leadership industry including: *Bad Leadership, The End of Leadership,* and *Professionalizing Leadership.*

In *The End of Leadership,* she describes how despite the countless leadership programs, courses, seminars, trainers, consultants and coaches claiming to teach people how to lead, there is "scant evidence" that this enormous investment of time and money has paid off. (The leadership development industry is estimated to be $15 billion annually in the U.S. and $50 billion worldwide.)

In her follow up book, *Professionalizing Leadership,* she notes that since the publishing of the End of Leadership in 2012, she is no longer alone in beginning to blow the whistle on these unethical practices such as trying to teach a complex and technical skill in a two-week seminar (which is what most of them do). "Since then, I have been joined by a small but fierce cadre of others who point to the yawning gap between what the leadership industry claims to do, and what it does."

Kellerman is joined by Stanford's Jeffrey Pfeffer as respected academics, thoughtful intellectuals, and true insiders who have recently turned leadership industry "whistleblowers."

Pfeffer, a prominent Stanford business school professor, and author of numerous books on management and leadership, including *Leadership BS: Fixing Workplaces and Careers One Truth at a Time,* writes "The single biggest barrier to effective leadership is, in my view, the leadership industry itself. Instead of telling people the skills and behaviors they need to be effective in getting things done, we tell them almost the opposite– blandishments about how we wish people would be, and how we wish workplaces were."

He states flatly "The leadership industry has failed. It's not just that all the efforts to develop better leaders have failed to appreciably improve leadership, but they often make things much worse."

Pfeffer writes, "If one is at all sensitive to the human costs incurred as leaders flame out and lose their jobs, cares and concerns that I and I suspect many others share, then the continuing failure of the leadership industry in all of its forms and activities to make things better needs to be both explained and remedied."

Finally, leadership researcher and New York Times bestselling author Duff McDonald describes the leadership industry this way, "Most of it is bullshit. Unfortunately, there are few business school faculty who could ever summon the courage to admit such a thing. But some do, and using the same language."

For our purposes here, I want to highlight three crucial facts in this whole sordid affair that is the leadership training and coaching industry.

First, the vast majority of so-called leadership experts, trainers and coaches do not know the answers to the most basic questions about leadership: what is leadership, how does it work, and how can you develop it?

Second, as I explained above, none of the leadership experts can agree on which approach or style works best. In fact, about 90% of experts will tell you that the style they advocate is the "best" style and should pretty much be used with all people and circumstances.

Finally, as I mentioned already and will explain in more detail later in this book, the reason that the experts can't agree on the above fundamentals is because they are "subject to their own worldview bias." I will explain this in more detail later, but this essentially, it means that they are unaware of their assumptions and biases about human psychology, human motivation, and follower's needs and behavior.

My colleagues and I, under the guidance of my mentor Ken Wilber, were the first to notice (and teach and write about) this pattern. This pattern, definitively explains why there are so many definitions and descriptions of "effective" leadership that wildly contradict each other to the point of being often mutually exclusive.

This is why, as you will see shortly, worldviews are right at the center of my model. And the different leadership approaches (or styles as they can be called) that each of the four worldviews expects from legitimate and credible leaders (in their eyes) is also at the center of my model. This is what makes it universal.

Rather than a one-size-fits-all approach that amounts to pushing one's unconscious worldview bias, the new approach described in this book accounts for different follower worldviews, needs and preferences, and accounts for the four universal leadership styles seen in nearly all leadership theory literature and leadership research.

My "Universal Leadership Model," explained in detail in a later chapter, is the first model that connects these four universal worldviews with the four universal leadership styles. This connection forms the heart of the *"Unifying Theory of Leadership"* that I developed with Ken Wilber at the Integral Institute.

This "meta theory" of leadership explains which leadership approach (or style) will work with which people and circumstances, and what approaches will be disastrous with which people and circumstances.

My *Practice-based Leadership Development* methodology, which I will explain in detail in a later chapter, is also unique in that it is the first to break down the technical and complex skill of leadership into three "essential abilities" and nine essential leadership practices, and then proceeds to train leaders using "Deliberate Practice" which comes from the field of Expert Performance Theory, developed by Anders Ericsson.

In the next chapter, *The Leadership Rosetta Stone,* I outline the four different definitions of "effective leadership" that the four different camps of leadership advice- givers offer (which reflect their unconscious worldview bias).

For now, it is useful to offer a stripped down, you could say generic or "worldview agnostic" definition, free of worldview bias.

> *Leadership: the ability or activity of inspiring and/or influencing people in relationship, over time, toward shared goals.*

The word "leadership" implies a trust-based relationship over time with shared goals, and the word "follower" implies voluntary (consensual) participation. Remember that followership is voluntary. A follower chooses to see a person as their leader, and that can be revoked (by the follower) at any time. A follower offers discretionary effort, that is effort above and beyond what would be considered compliance, in the case of an authority figure compelling them to comply with their order.

So when influence occurs within the context of a leader-follower relationship, the follower is voluntarily participating in being influenced. Put another way, followers actually want the leader to influence them. Followers give the leader consent to influence them.

Bringing all of this together, we can think of "leadership influence" as *affecting a follower in such a way that they voluntarily change how they think or behave.*

The next big idea I want to highlight in this introduction lies at the very heart of why 80% of leadership development efforts fail, and why so much of leadership theory and so much leadership advice, is so utterly bogus.

This may strike you as a little bit provocative, controversial, or, in the worst case even condescending. But it's really none of those things if you hear me out and grasp the nuance of the reality that I'm pointing out for you.

So, bear with me and you will be glad that you did. Many leadership trainers and coaches talk about leadership as if it is about personality traits, or qualities, or vague concepts like EQ (more on this later). While these topics are interesting in the background, discussing them does next to nothing to help leaders actually improve their leadership performance.

Many leadership trainers and coaches talk about leadership as if it is about personality traits, or qualities or vague concepts like EQ (more on this later). While these topics are interesting in the background, discussing them does next to nothing to help leaders actually improve their leadership performance. Improving leadership performance has little to do with concepts and everything to do with skill. The vast majority of leadership trainers and coaches seem to be ignorant of the relatively obvious and definitely indisputable fact that leadership is a technical and complex skill.

> *There is only one way to learn a technical and / or complex skill. That is to train in the specific, requisite techniques until they are internalized as habits, then layer on more techniques to create skills, then combine several new skills to create new "skill sets" and ultimately those skill sets mature into what we call "abilities."*

This crucial point is a central element in my rapid leadership development methodology called "Accelerating Leadership," that is the subject of Chapter 4. To get better at leadership, you must understand the nature of leadership. Leadership is not a set of personality traits and it is not some vague concept (although many authors, trainers and coaches speak about it as though it is).

> *Leadership is a technical and complex skill, no different from all the many other technical and complex skills you have already learned both as a child and as an adult.*

You know this intuitively, but for some odd reason, most leadership authors, trainers and coaches don't seem to.

Learning the technical and complex skill of leadership is no different than learning any of those other technical and complex skills that you already taken the time to learn. The method is exactly the same. Yet less than 10% of leadership development programs use it.

Learning leadership is exactly the same as learning to play a musical instrument, mastering a martial art or sport, flying an airplane or any other technical and/or complex skill. How could it be otherwise?

To "reinvent leadership" we must first face the stark reality that leadership, like every other technical and complex skill we have already learned in our lives, is comprised of skills and those skills are, in turn, comprised of techniques (that can also be referred to as "practices").

Any proposed explanation of leadership that fails to point to the techniques and practices that comprise the technical and complex skill called "leadership" is flawed from the start. And this is why about 90% of models, frameworks and explanations offered by leadership advice-givers are bogus.

This is such an important point, I am going to revisit it several times in this book coming at it from a variety of different angles and using different analogies. Please pardon my deliberate repetition, but if there is one thing you must understand, it is this. And I don't want you to just be familiar with it as a concept, I want you to believe it and understand it in your bones. Once you do, all of your future leadership development efforts (and the efforts in your organization) will be much easier and more effective. This is one of the main things I want you to get out of this book.

Let me illustrate this crucial point in very concrete terms that I hope you can relate to on a personal level. I will refer to several other common technical and complex skills that you may have already learned.

Learning Guitar

No one in their right mind would try to learn to play an instrument, try to learn a martial art, or try to learn to fly an airplane the way 90% of leadership development programs train leadership. Can you imagine trying to learn to play the guitar by reading case studies of great guitar players in history, or worse, hearing stories about the accomplishments of great guitarists, or worse still, reading a list of character traits of these men and women?

Learning a Martial Art

Can you imagine trying to learn Kung Fu by hearing stories about Bruce Lee, and descriptions of his personality traits or by merely adopting his mindset or philosophy?

As absurd as this sounds, it is even more absurd that this is exactly what approximately 90% of leadership development programs are doing in the $15 billion-a-year leadership development industry (in the United States alone).

My team and I have been creating and delivering successful leadership development programs for over two decades, and I am now calling out these bogus industry practices. Research shows clearly that programs that emphasize leadership qualities, traits, philosophy, and case studies (instead of techniques and practices) fail to help leaders improve their leadership skills or their leadership performance.

Learning Piano

I want you to pause for a moment and imagine signing up your son or daughter to a training to learn to play piano and asking them what techniques your child will be practicing each week. Now imagine that their answer is, "Our students don't practice any specific techniques. Our students study the stories and personality traits of great piano players."

There is an entire field called "Complex Skill Instructional Design." Google it.

It is a very well-known fact in training and development that in order to learn any technical or complex skill, you must break the overall ability down into specific skill sets and skills, and then down to the techniques that make up those skills.

This is common sense. You already know this.

Sports Such as Baseball or Basketball

Consider the technical and complex skill called baseball. Many children learn this complex skill. Perhaps you did. When you (or your child, niece or nephew) learned the ability to play baseball, it was broken down to *throwing, catching, hitting the ball, and running the bases.* In the case of basketball, it is *dribbling, passing, shooting* and *rebounding.* In the case of mixed martial arts, it is *wrestling, kick-boxing* and *grappling.*

There is also a well-known field called "Expert Performance Theory" or "Deliberate Practice" (as it is better known). You have no doubt heard of "10,000 hours" as the estimated amount of time it takes for a person practicing deliberately to go from beginner to expert level in any complex skill.

Why don't leadership development programs incorporate "Deliberate Practice" into their efforts and teach their students the practices (the techniques and skills) that leaders need to be effective?

My partners, colleagues and I have been teaching the complex skill called "leadership" using "complex skill instructional design" and "deliberate practice" for more than 20 years. I have logged more than 20,000 hours doing precisely that. So, let me save you a lot of time, energy, money and heartburn and tell you what does not work and exactly what does actually work for leadership development.

I summarize what works in this introduction and will unpack each of these ideas in different chapters within the book.

Leadership, like any other complex skill, is made up of a specific set of skills with discrete, concrete behaviors that can be practiced, repeated, and internalized as habits.

Again, using baseball as a familiar example, you have to be able to throw, hit, run, and do several other skills before you have the ability that we call "baseball." The same goes for martial arts, music, flying an airplane and leadership.

> *There is only one way to learn a complex skill: practice and internalize a technique, then combine several techniques (in layers) over time.*

This is called "complex skill instructional design" and "deliberate practice." It involves breaking the broader ability down into smaller skill sets and skills, then teaching those specific techniques and behaviors.

Clearly, to learn (or improve) this ability called leadership, it must be broken down into specific skill sets and discrete techniques (behaviors).

Think about mixed martial arts (MMA). There are three major abilities (*wrestling, striking* and *grappling*) and each is made up of a dozen or so techniques. The fact that MMA athletes have separate training and separate coaches for wrestling, striking and grappling underscores the nature of this complex ability (which has many parallels to leadership, which is obviously at least as complex as martial arts).

I will now summarize why I think the leadership development industry is not developing leaders.

1. Most leadership trainers and coaches do not recognize leadership as a technical and complex skill, and instead, speak about leader character traits (or qualities as they often call them).

2. Most leadership trainers and coaches focus primarily or even exclusively on the leader and under-emphasize or completely

ignore the leadership context (the specific circumstances that will call for different approaches).

3. Most leadership trainers and coaches under-emphasize or completely ignore the followers, their worldviews (values, beliefs, assumptions), their specific needs, and their preferences for the kind of leadership they will resonate with

4. Most leadership advice-givers make "one-size-fits-all" pronouncements that this is the "best way" to lead with all followers in all circumstances. Any leadership advice that fails to provide guidelines for which people and circumstances this method will work with is bad advice because no leadership approach will work with all follower types and in all circumstances.

5. Most leadership advice is based on a very rudimentary and unsophisticated understanding of psychology. Very few advice-givers have a working knowledge of Positive Psychology, Interpersonal Psychology, Developmental Psychology or Integral Psychology—all of which are essential to make sense of such a complex field as organizational leadership.

I can summarize all of this by saying that the vast majority of so-called "leadership experts" in today's leadership development industry do not know what leadership actually is, can't explain to customers how leadership actually works, and certainly do not understand how to develop this complex and technical skill (that they don't even recognize as such).

I will reserve an in-depth analysis of what is badly wrong with the leadership development industry for my book, *Blowing the Whistle on Bogus Leadership: Veteran Industry Insider Reveals Why the Leadership Development Industry is Not Developing Leaders.*

Now that we have discussed what makes so much leadership advice bogus, we will transition into a description of a series of astonishing breakthroughs that have occurred in recent years that will allow us to actually reinvent leadership in the coming years.

The beginning of these breakthroughs occurred in the early 2000s at the Stagen Leadership Academy that I co-founded and at Ken Wilber's Integral Institute (where I was the head of the Business and Leadership Center). After over a million dollars in research and development costs over a ten-year period, we ultimately found the key to unlock our elusive "unifying theory of leadership" which revealed the pattern that connects all leadership theories, and explains which leadership approaches will work with which people and circumstances (and which will fail with which people and circumstances). We dubbed the discovery "The Leadership Rosetta Stone," the topic of the next chapter.

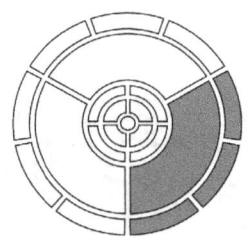

CHAPTER 2:
THE LEADERSHIP ROSETTA STONE

The Rosetta Stone is an ancient Egyptian artifact on which the same information is inscribed in: Egyptian hieroglyphs, Demotic, and Greek. The discovery of the Rosetta Stone allowed researchers to decode the language of Egyptian hieroglyphs for the first time in history. This term "Rosetta Stone" is often used idiomatically to describe any critical key that unlocks something previously difficult (or impossible) to decipher. After reviewing hundreds of leadership texts, including most of the popular books on leadership theory and practice, an unmistakable pattern emerged for me and my research team at The Integral Institute (under the mentorship of Ken Wilber) and the Stagen Leadership Academy.Nearly all "leadership theory" texts and books that claim to explain the "best" way to lead describe the writers' subjective ideas about which leadership tactics work best with followers based on their own assumptions about the world and the people being led. All of the texts that described the authors' opinions about which leadership techniques/approaches work best with followers are based on their assumptions about the world and the people being led.

With rare exceptions, the authors' inherent assumptions about the world and people (and biases for which approaches should be used) lined up with the four "worldviews" I had learned about from Ken Wilber, Jean Gebser, Robert Kegan and the other developmental psychologists I had studied or worked with.

This turned out to be the key to unlocking the Universal Theory of Leadership. When we group the leadership theories, approaches, techniques and tools by the worldview of their advocate, we see that in most cases, those methods do work well for followers who share that worldview. Integral theory provides us with an easy way (if you know what to look for) to identify follower mindsets, or worldviews.

Therefore, if we know a follower's worldview, we will know with a great deal of accuracy which leadership styles and approaches will be most resonant with them, that they will feel drawn to, will trust, willingly follow, and the leader for whom they will happily offer their "discretionary effort."

Next, I will first summarize the four most common worldviews most relevant in organizational life in the developed world and briefly introduce the four universal leadership styles and show how you apply them to the three essential leadership abilities and nine leadership core competencies.

The Four Universal Worldviews

In a later section of this book entitled "Values Research," I will provide a detailed description of decades of values and worldviews research that demonstrates that nearly all major theorists (who study values and worldviews) agree that there are four universal worldviews, and nearly all also agree on their common names). For now, I will keep the discussion brief and simply introduce the Four Universal Worldviews that are essential building blocks for our Leadership Rosetta Stone.

These four worldviews should be familiar to you by now as I introduced them previously when I explained the four leadership paradigms.

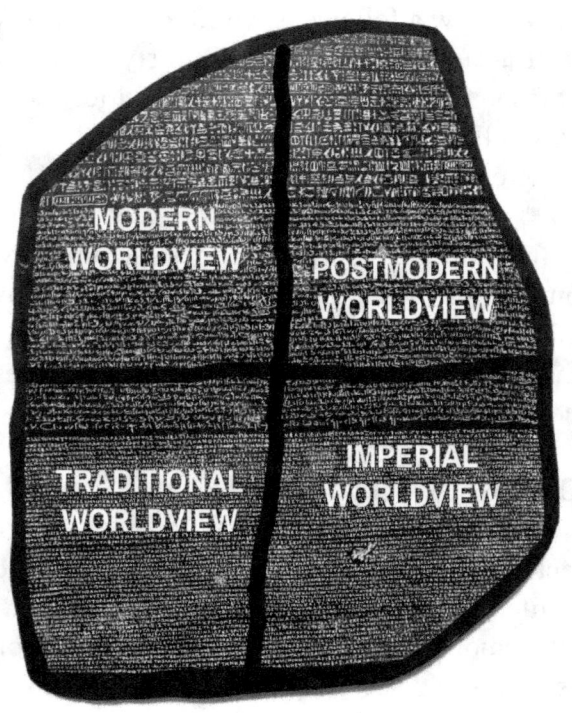

The Imperial Worldview

The Imperial worldview first emerged in society during the time of feudal kingdoms and is roughly equivalent to the Bronze Age and is still very much alive and well today. People with this worldview see the world as made up of "predators and prey", where the strongest and most cunning survive, gain power, and satisfy their wants. They tend to be fiercely independent living by their "own rules" and are disinterested in conforming to many social norms, are driven to break free from limits, achieve their goals, or impose their will. People with this worldview tend to believe the best way to think and behave is "my way." People with an *Imperial* worldview find the *Autocratic* leadership style most credible.

The Traditional Worldview

The Traditional worldview initially emerged historically with the monotheistic religious traditions and the Roman Empire, and we see it starting with the Iron Age (and continuing through the Middle Ages.) People with this worldview see the world as an ordered existence under the control of a higher authority and ultimate truth. They tend to see the world in a concrete, literal, and dualistic manner: right vs. wrong, good vs. evil, and so on. They emphasize social stability and "mainstream" morality. People with this worldview tend to believe that there is only one right way to think and behave. People with a *Traditional* worldview will find the *Authority* style most credible.

The Modern Worldview

The Modern Age emerged during the historical western enlightenment and the dawn of scientific thinking we associate with "The Renaissance", which eventually led to the Industrial Age. People with this worldview tend to believe in the advancement of humankind through the application of the rational mind and its scientific, technological, and medical manifestations. Life is to be met and mastered by finding the best way to act on its limitless opportunities. People with this worldview tend to believe that while there are many valid ways to think and behave, there is always one best way. People with *Modern* worldview will find the *Strategic* leadership style most credible.

The Postmodern Worldview

The Postmodern worldview first emerged in the 1960s with the advent of computer technology, networking and globalization and we associate it with the Information Age. People with this worldview believe the world is a diverse web of interrelationships where life forms depend on each other for survival, and there is no single explanatory system (view of reality) that can account for all the phenomena of life; rather there are many truths. People with this worldview tend to believe that there are many valid ways to think and behave but that there is no real way to judge the superiority of one way or another. People with *Postmodern* worldview will find the *Humanistic* leadership style most credible.

Now that we have initially defined the four worldviews, we will look at the four "universal leadership styles" that must be paired with people who share these corresponding worldviews in order to be viewed as a credible leader in the eyes of your followers.

The Four Universal Leadership Styles

To aid in the learning process, I will first provide a "fly over" with the four very brief definitions and descriptions of the four universal leadership styles that provide a hub that the Universal Leadership Model spins around.

Autocratic Leadership: The person with the most power leads via command and control. In short, this leadership style is based on power and control.

Authority Leadership: The person with positional authority leads via chain of command. In short, this leadership style is based on rules and compliance.

Strategic Leadership: The person with the most expertise leads via strategic planning and tangible incentives. In short, this leadership style is based on expertise and winning.

Humanistic Leadership: Leadership is not vested in any one person; rather, it emerges from the inclusive collective via consensus in the service of the greater good. In short, this leadership style is based on inclusivity, equality and consensus.

Now that you have a basic idea of what these four styles are, I will elaborate on the simple definitions and add a more detailed description of each style.

Autocratic Leadership

Simple definition: The person with the most power leads via command and control.

Approach: This style reflects a "Unilateral" approach to leadership. When using this style, leaders impose their will through reputation, fear and respect, tightly control information and choices, reward compliance and punish disloyalty. The oldest of the styles, is the way you would expect a ruler (such as a king or dictator) to "rule" their subjects. It is still extremely popular today (both with some rules and also with a surprisingly large percentages of followers and also voters).

Appreciated by: People with predominantly Imperial worldviews who respect dominance and aggression, and who prefer to follow leaders who are perceived as being the strongest, toughest, and most dominant who will be able to protect them from (or defeat) their enemies. Another word for leaders who use this style is "strongman" leaders.

Authority Leadership

This is also known as "Authority" leadership, "chain of command" leadership, and "authoritarian" leadership.

Simple definition: The person with positional authority leads via chain of command.

Approach: This style reflects a "Hierarchical" approach to leadership. When using this style, leaders compel followers to dutifully comply with the established protocols, coordinate efforts and meet requirements prescribed by authority. This style is the most "parental" of all the styles; the leader is in a position of "parent" and followers are in the position of "child."

Appreciated by: People with Traditional worldviews who value honor, service, loyalty, and conformity, and share traditional beliefs and a willingness to sacrifice now for future rewards... and who prefer to follow leaders who are perceived as having positional and/or moral authority.

Strategic Leadership

This is also known as "Expert Leadership." Some academics who are strongly biased toward the next style (Humanistic) will refer to this style as "Transactional leadership."

Simple definition: The person with the most expertise leads via strategic planning and tangible incentives.

Approach: This style reflects a "Transactional" approach to leadership. When using this style, leaders leverage financial incentives to motivate teams to execute strategic plans in order to outperform competitors.

Appreciated by: People with a Modern worldview who seek opportunities to advance toward their individual goals and who prefer to follow leaders who are perceived as having the most expertise and ability to achieve goals.

Humanistic Leadership

This is also known as "Inclusive leadership," "Transformational Leadership," "Collaborative leadership," and "Self-Managed Teams" (the members lead themselves).

Simple definition: Leadership is not vested in any one person; rather, it emerges from the inclusive collective via consensus in the service of the greater good.

Approach: This style reflects a "Transformational" approach to leadership. When using this style, leaders strive for inclusiveness and a feeling of equality by inviting people's feelings and intuition via dialog to arrive at consensus. This style attempts to draw out the "human potential" of their followers and work together collaboratively toward common goals. This approach strongly favors "self-managed teams" over "single-leader led teams."

Appreciated by: People with a Postmodern worldview who value diversity, equality, and inclusivity (known as D.E.I.), authenticity, connection, opportunity for personal growth and contribution to the collective, and who prefer to follow leaders who are perceived as being aware, sensitive to the well-being of others, who strive for consensus, and who always treats others as equals.

Pairing Leadership Styles with Follower Worldviews

Followers with an *Imperial* worldview will find Autocratic leadership credible. These followers look for a leader who is perceived to be powerful and who can protect them from and/or defeat their enemies. If you use any of the other three styles with a person with an Imperial worldview, you run the risk of undermining your credibility with these types of followers.

People with a *Traditional* worldview will find Authority leadership credible. These followers are looking for a leader who is perceived to have "moral" or positional authority (and the "morals" in this case will always be defined by traditional values and/or traditional religious beliefs. Again, if you use any of the other three styles with a person with a Traditional worldview, you run the risk of undermining your credibility because they won't see you as a legitimate leader (according to what they look for in a leader).

People with a *Modern* worldview will find Strategic leadership credible. These followers are looking for the leader to be the person with the most expertise who is most likely able to help them achieve their goals. Again, if you use any of the other three styles with a person with a Modern worldview, you run the risk of undermining your credibility as you don't exhibit the qualities (and the approaches) that they associate with credible leaders and competent leadership.

People with a *Postmodern* worldview will find Humanistic leadership credible. These followers are looking for the leader to treat everyone as an equal and who strives for equality and consensus. Again, if you use any of the other three styles with a person with a Postmodern worldview, you run the risk of undermining your credibility, as they may not see you as a legitimate leader (they might use the phrase "conscious leader").

The Theorists Are Also Subject to Their Worldviews

By now you are starting to recognize the pattern. The four universal worldviews track perfectly with the four widely acknowledged "paradigms of leadership" put forth by the different experts. As I will explain in this book, the theorists who put forth leadership theories are often subject to their own worldview biases. The advocates of the different approaches (or styles of leadership) can be seen clearly to hold these different worldviews. In most cases their bias is unconscious and they do not admit or acknowledge the existence of the other three worldviews. And they certainly don't agree that the other leadership paradigms (other than the one they are biased towards) hold any merit at all. This is of course ridiculous and reflects the fact that they are leaving out the context dimension of leadership. Perhaps most embarrassing of all, many so-called leadership experts and leadership training programs seem to leave out followers altogether! Even many of the most respected leadership authorities have overlooked this pattern that the follower's mindset (worldview) determines, in large part, which "leadership paradigm" will offer the most utility in that context.

This chapter has introduced you to Integral Leadership. This is an important topic that warrants a much longer treatment. If this interests you, see my book, *Integral Leadership: The World's First Unifying Theory of Leadership That Will Forever Transform How You Understand, Practice and Develop Leadership*

We are now ready to assemble the "Universal Leadership Model!" As a way to help you not only fully understand the model but also to appreciate the relationships between its different components, I will walk you through a logical, step-by-step process of building the model section-by-section in the next chapter.

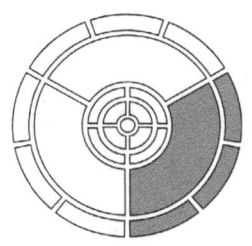

CHAPTER 3:
THE UNIVERSAL LEADERSHIP MODEL

When we combine the "Leadership Rosetta Stone", which clearly articulates four distinct approaches to leadership, with the three "Inherent Leadership Responsibilities" and the nine "Essential Leadership Skills", you have what I call the "Universal Leadership Model." All leaders everywhere, regardless of context, share these three inherent leadership responsibilities. All leaders fulfill their responsibilities by engaging in the activities we see under each of the nine leadership skill sets (also called "core competencies"). Naturally, the activities, techniques and skills may use different names, but the work of leadership is universal, and the skills leaders need to be effective are also universal.

What is different from culture to culture and leader to leader is the "approach" or the "style" with which they undertake these activities.

A leader can engage the activities associated with each skill set using any of the four universal leadership styles: *Autocratic, Authority, Strategic,* and *Humanistic,* which track perfectly with the four predominant leadership paradigms we explored previously.

While this may sound quite straightforward, my colleagues and I are the only ones who are approaching leadership and leadership development in this uniquely effective way.

Our *Universal Leadership Model* is an "integrally-informed" approach to leadership. In the year 2000, I created a one-year training program called "The Integral Leadership Program" and launched a leadership academy with my close friend Rand Stagen to bring this approach to the business world with the goal of helping to "make business a force for good." As of this writing, more than two thousand companies (and growing) have adopted this approach.

This "integral" or "conscious" approach to leadership played a central role in helping to launch and grow the "Conscious Capitalism" movement (also known as the "Conscious Business Movement). I mention this to highlight the fact that this is not merely a model or framework. This approach to leadership and leadership development that is not "theoretical;" rather, it is tried and proven to be extraordinarily effective over more than two decades with thousands of companies including non-profit companies and other types of organizations around the world, even in developing countries. Many people familiar with the field of leadership development believe that this approach is one of the most effective, if not <u>the</u> most effective approach to leadership development that exists.

In this chapter we will assemble the "Universal Leadership Model" from the components we have already introduced: 1) The Leadership Rosetta Stone, 2) Inherent Leadership Responsibilities and 3) Leadership Core Competencies. For clarity's sake, I will bring one element in at a time, illustrate each, and then combine them as we assemble the model.

First, recall the four universal leadership styles: *Strategic, Humanistic, Authority,* and *Autocratic.*

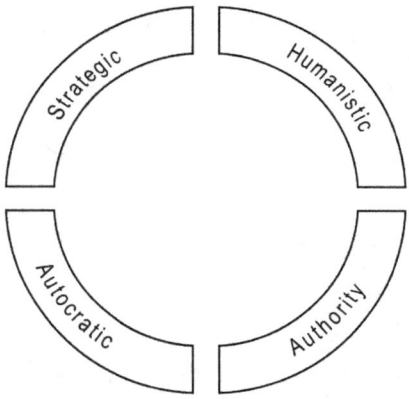

Next, the *Leadership Rosetta Stone* revealed the four predominant "follower worldviews." And we learned that each worldview has a specific definition of legitimate leadership and is looking for very different things in people who they view as credible leaders.

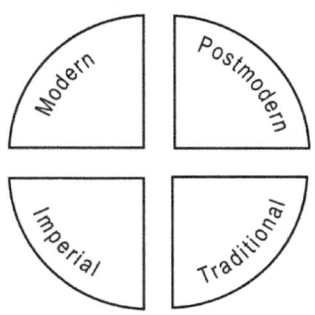

We now recognize that for leadership to be viewed as effective (by those being led), the correct leadership style must be paired with the follower's worldview (which dictates how they define effective leadership and what they look for in a credible leader. When we bring the styles and the worldviews together, we can illustrate it like this.

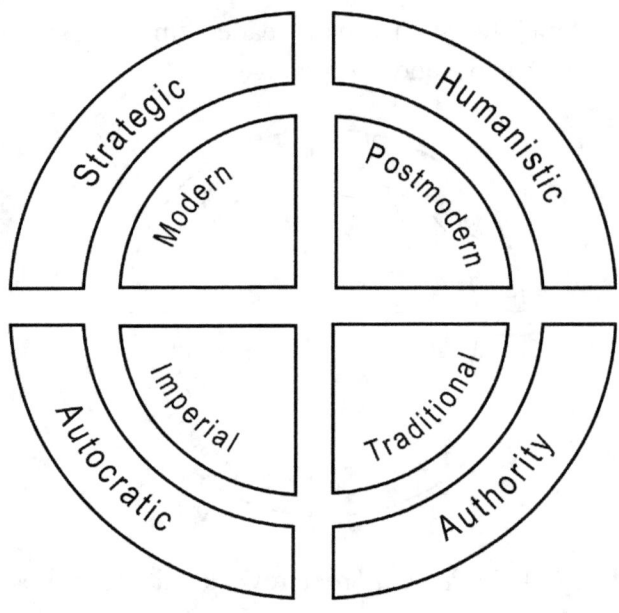

In the above illustration we can see that the correct leadership style is paired with the worldview of the follower (according to the style of leadership that follower will view as credible and legitimate).

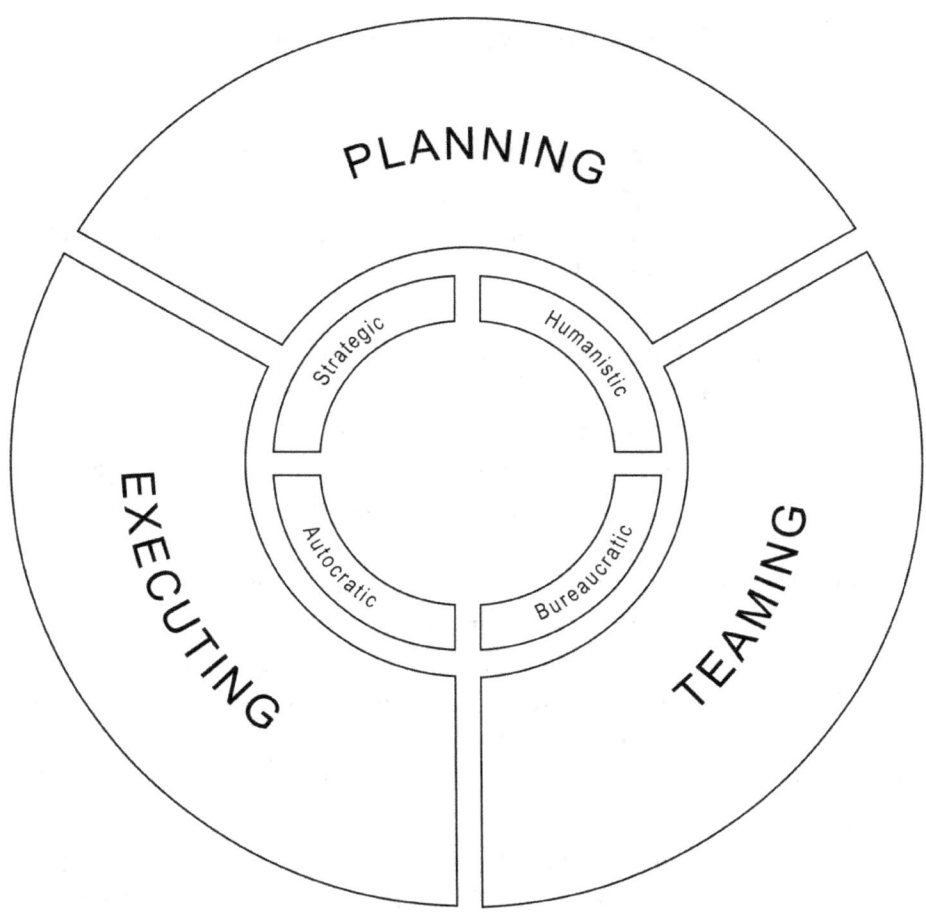

Next, you will recall that there are three "Inherent Leadership Responsibilities," which point to the three "Essential Abilities" all leaders must possess to be considered competent and adequately well-rounded leaders.

Using common terms, those are often referred to as *Planning, Teaming* and *Executing*. I introduce additional, more nuanced terms in Chapter 4: Accelerating Leadership.

When you take into account the leadership style, you can see that different types of leaders will take a different approach, that is, use a different style as they fulfill these responsibilities. Put another way, all leaders demonstrate three essential abilities, but they use different styles.

For example, one leader may use a "Humanistic" approach to *planning, teaming* and *executing*. Another leader may use an "Autocratic" approach, another a "Strategic" approach and another a "Authority" approach.

This fact is reflected in our illustration with the four different styles pictured inside the three responsibilities. While this is a static illustration, you might want to imagine the center circle (with the leadership styles) spinning around so that different styles can be deployed with different areas of responsibilities.

Sadly, some leaders lack any versatility at all, and always use their native style (example: Strategic) with all followers. The result of only using one style is that it is only resonant with those followers who have that corresponding worldview (values and beliefs). For the other estimated 25-75% of the people in typical diverse organizations (who have a different worldview), that leader's style comes across as ineffective, out of touch, lame, not trustworthy, clueless or even foolish. Imagine how ridiculous the positional, "parental," authoritarian style comes across to postmodern followers who despise hierarchy and believe that legitimate leaders always treat everyone as equals. Get it?

Versatile leaders (this includes all leaders who have had the benefit of my Integral Leadership training) develop much-needed capacity to switch their style up and emphasize different leadership styles with different people and circumstances, as the situation warrants. For example, they can adopt a more Strategic style with their modern worldview, goal-oriented, success-driven followers, and then they lean on a more Humanistic style with their postmodern worldview, progressive followers who expect to be treated as an equal (and expect their feelings and perspectives to be respected and taken into account on all major organizational decisions). And that same versatile leader will adopt a more "hierarchical" Authority approach with their Traditional worldview followers who see legitimate leaders as using their positional authority to enforce rules and compliance.

Next, you will recall that for each of the inherent leadership responsibilities, that leaders engage a variety of practices, activities, skill sets and/or "competencies" to fulfill their responsibilities. In our pragmatic framework, we describe three skill sets for each of the three responsibilities (3 skill sets x 3 responsibilities = 9 total skill sets).

Each of these nine skill sets consist of about half a dozen techniques (behaviors, not concepts). I go into much more detail about these techniques in my other books. This book focuses on the "*Teamwork & Culture*" dimension.

This next simplified illustration shows the three essential abilities (in the middle area) along with the nine skill sets around the outer ring).

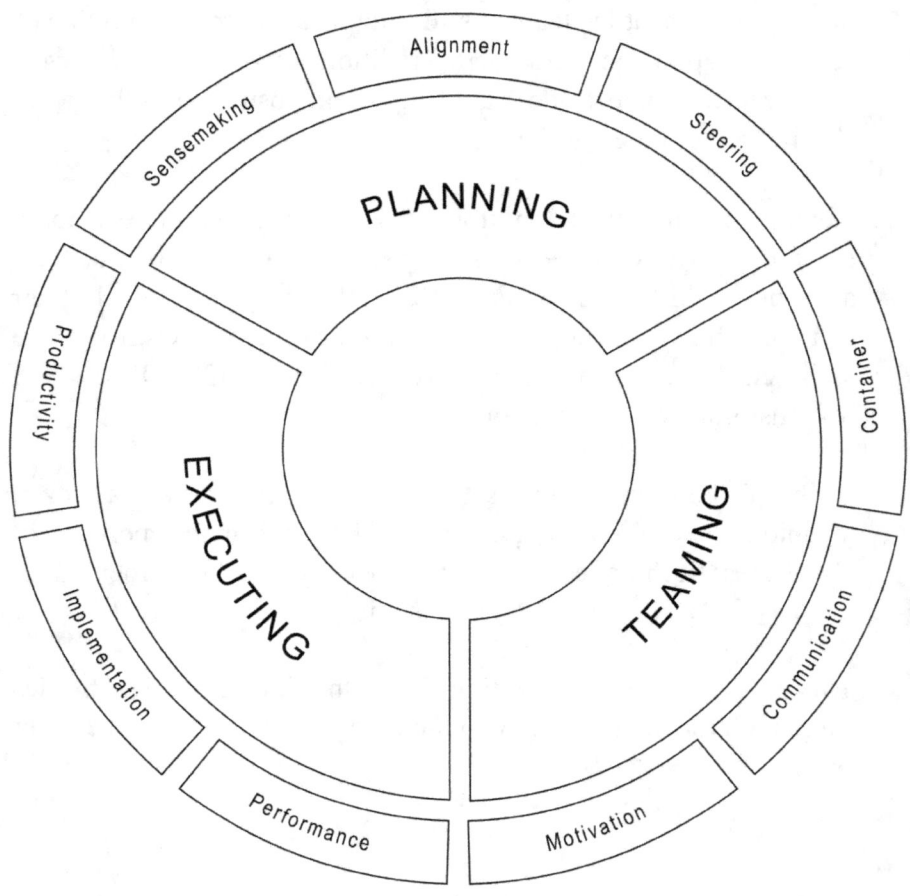

Next, we will want to bring the four leadership styles and four follower worldviews back into our illustration. This way, our illustration reflects that leaders can engage their three "essential abilities" (*planning, teaming* and *executing*) in the middle of the diagram, along with their corresponding (3x3) skill sets along the outer ring using any of these leadership styles, and those styles should be paired up correctly based on the followers being led.

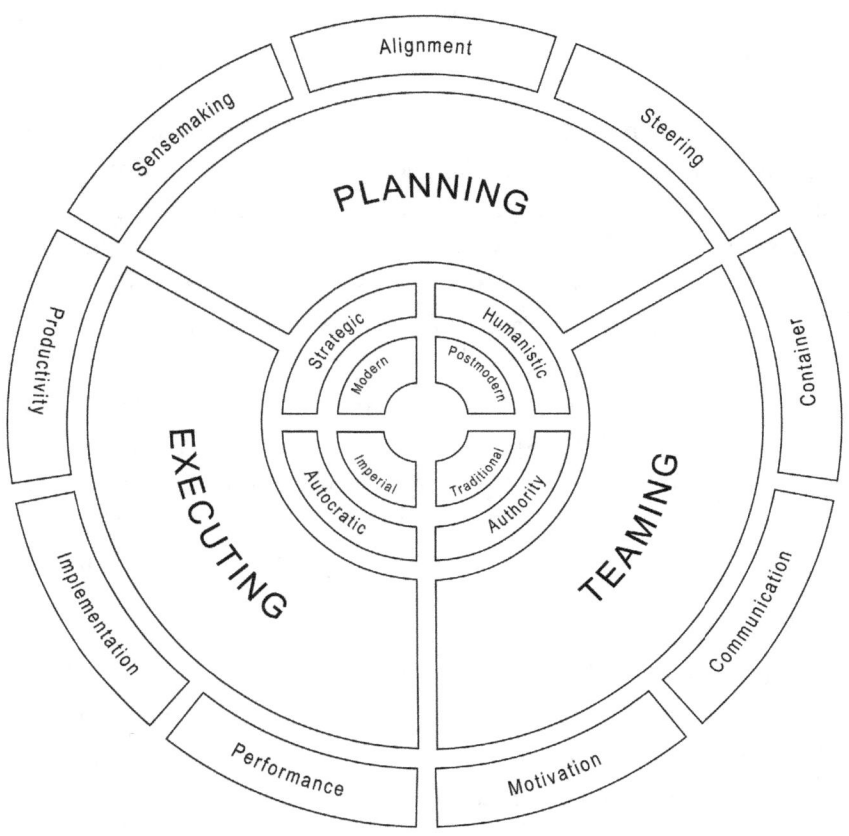

Like so. Now, this version of the model visually suggests that for each ability (middle section) and for each of the nine skill sets (outer section), there are four different styles to draw upon.

For example, there is a "Authority" way to hold people accountable for job performance and a "strategic" way to hold people accountable for their performance. There is an "autocratic" approach to creating the team "container" and there is a "humanistic" approach to creating a container (and they are as different as night and day). Similarly, there is a "humanistic" way to approach alignment around vision, for example, and there is a "strategic" way to approach coming up with the vision and aligning people around it. As a final example, there is an autocratic way to motivate people and teams, a authority way, and of course a more humanistic way.

Once you have experience working with this framework, you will realize it provides a nearly unlimited amount of versatility to the art and science of leadership. Mastering this approach will enable you to be an effective leader with a diverse population of followers. Eventually you will be able to influence, motivate, inspire and guide just about anyone, regardless of their worldview.

At first, this notion of leading with the requisite versatility of shifting from "Strategic" style to the "Humanistic" or "Authority" style appears difficult. Yet, my 22 years of teaching leaders to do this shows that it is actually easier than it looks. It just takes instruction from someone who knows this framework, and a lot of practice.

Simply put, to expand your versatility, you will need to select the next style you want to master, find a role model to emulate (and/or read my other books or take one of my many courses), and then practice the new style until it feels natural.

Here is a slightly longer instruction on how to do this.

Recall that the three most common worldviews in most organizations are *Traditional, Modern* and *Postmodern*. The good news is you already have one style down, I call that one your "native style." It is likely either Strategic or Humanistic (that pairs with the Modern and Postmodern follower worldviews respectively). If your role models were highly traditional, then maybe your native style is Authority (also called Authoritarian). That hierarchical style must only be used with followers with Traditional worldviews. (The other types of followers will find that "parental" approach quite off-putting, especially the postmodern types who hate hierarchy and expect legitimate leaders to treat everyone as an equal.)

Now, after you identify your "native" style, reflect on your team, organization and the followers you interact with the most.

In this example, I will assume your native style is Strategic. Well, you certainly have all the followers in your organization who have a Modern worldview covered.

What's the next largest group?

Is it Postmodern? If you work in tech or with a younger workforce (millennials and Gen Z) then you probably work with a lot of followers with the postmodern worldview. So then the "Humanistic" style is the one you want to master next!

The best way to learn that style (besides taking one of my courses) is to identify other leaders in your organization, and teachers and mentors, who are "fluent in that values dialect" and who either use the Humanistic style natively or have mastered it through practice.

Study them, notice how they always say "we" and almost never say "I". Notice how they let everyone else speak <u>first</u> before they speak. (Autocratic and Authoritarian leaders would never do that.) Pay attention to how these "Humanistic" leaders demonstrate respect for everyone's perspective, how they treat everyone as their equal, and how they strive for consensus.

Also notice the way that they hold people accountable, delegate, give feedback, motivate, handle group decisions and just about every other leader responsibility and activity is undertaken in a slightly different way than you do (contrasting the Humanistic style with the Strategic style in this hypothetical example).

The details of their Humanistic style should be obvious now that I have given you the "leadership styles cheat codes" in the form of my Leadership Rosetta Stone). The answers are all around you,

you just needed to know what to look for. And now you know exactly what to look for.

Before we move on, there are still two more elements to represent in the "Universal Leadership Model" that we have started to assemble.

Can you guess what is still missing in our illustration so far?

We have covered *followers, leadership styles, leadership responsibilities* and *leadership skills*. Recall the element that our leadership industry whistleblowers from Harvard and Stanford (Keller and Pfeffer) point out that is often ignored. Perhaps you guessed it. Recall what Lewin ignored when he studied young children doing arts and crafts to create a model of corporate leadership styles.

Did you guess it?

It is "organizational context" (or what I also call "circumstances").

Whether or not a given leader and their style (or approach) will be effective is largely a function of the context (the circumstances). As history has shown us repeatedly, an incompetent, failed, and discredited leader in one context will be heralded as a brilliant successful leader in a different context (with a different audience). Or the opposite, a leader may be very successful in one context and a dismal failure in another.

So when we add organizational context (circumstances) to our Universal Leadership Model it looks like this.

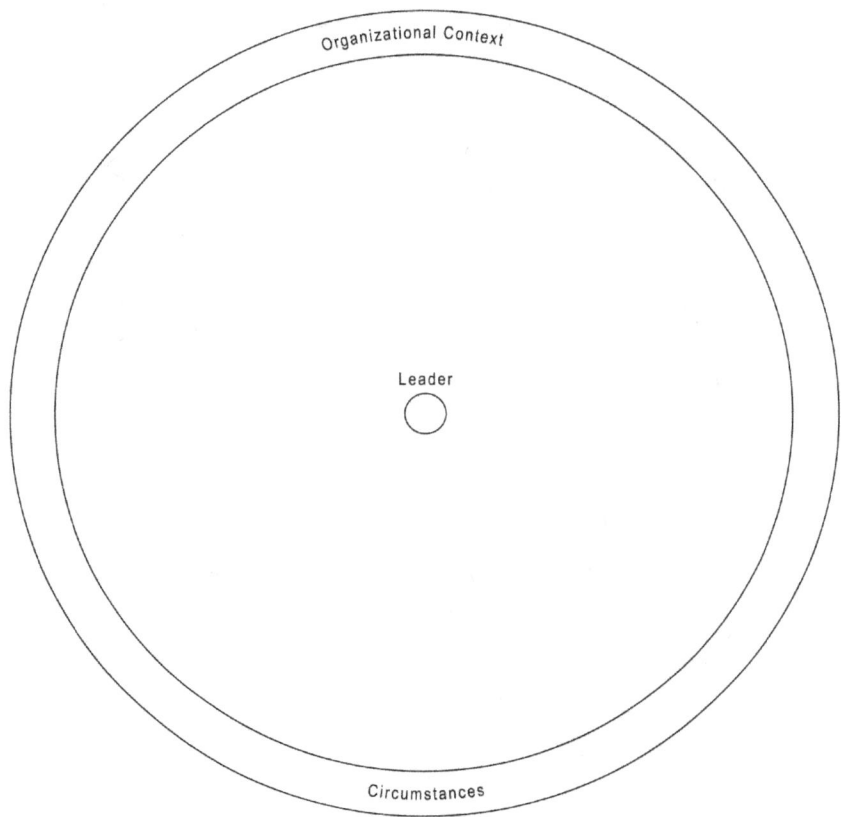

There is just one last element to add to our illustration. This last element, the leader, bears special emphasis. In this illustration you can see the leader (represented by small circle in the middle).

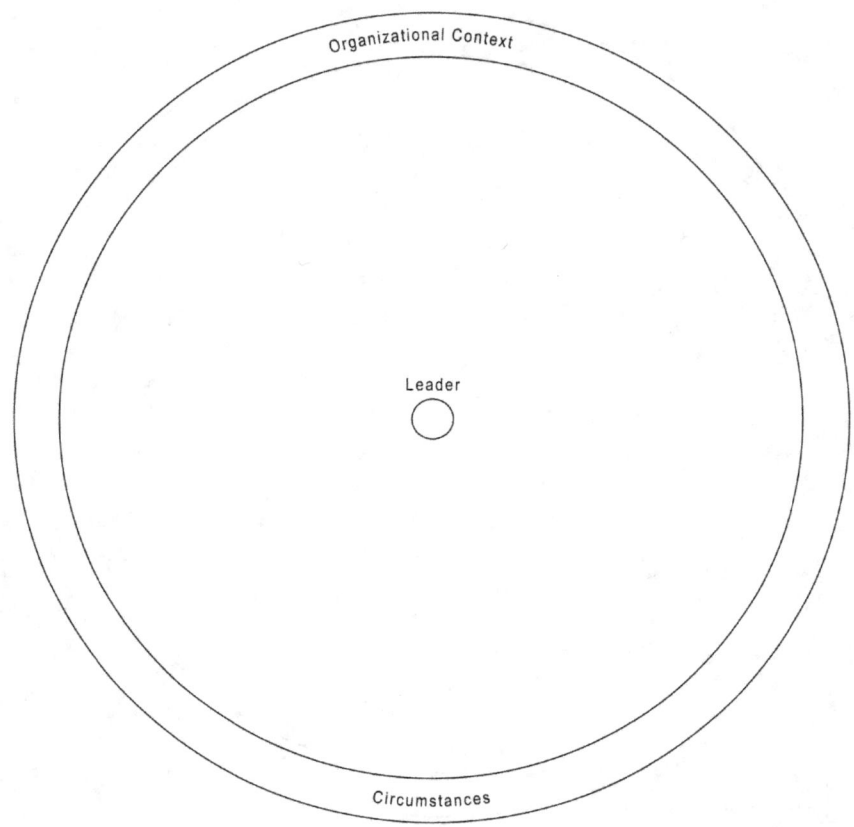

To be effective, this leader must first and foremost be able to make sense out of their circumstances. In many of our courses and coaching programs, we go into much detail about sensemaking. (You may recall it is one of the nine core competencies). Sensemaking is the leadership skill that leaders must draw upon to make sense of the context (their circumstances). In our leadership courses and coaching programs, we encourage leaders to ask the following questions:

What is really happening?
What is important?
What is needed?
And…
What is the most helpful action I can take?

The next important thing for a leader to understand after understanding the organizational context, is…

Who are the followers that they wish to influence (or lead)?

The most important thing about a follower's psychological makeup is their worldview because it determines which of the four universal leadership styles they will strongly prefer (and willingly follow). The next logical piece of the Universal Leadership Model to bring in will be the followers. The next logical piece of the Universal Leadership Model to bring in will be the <u>followers</u>."

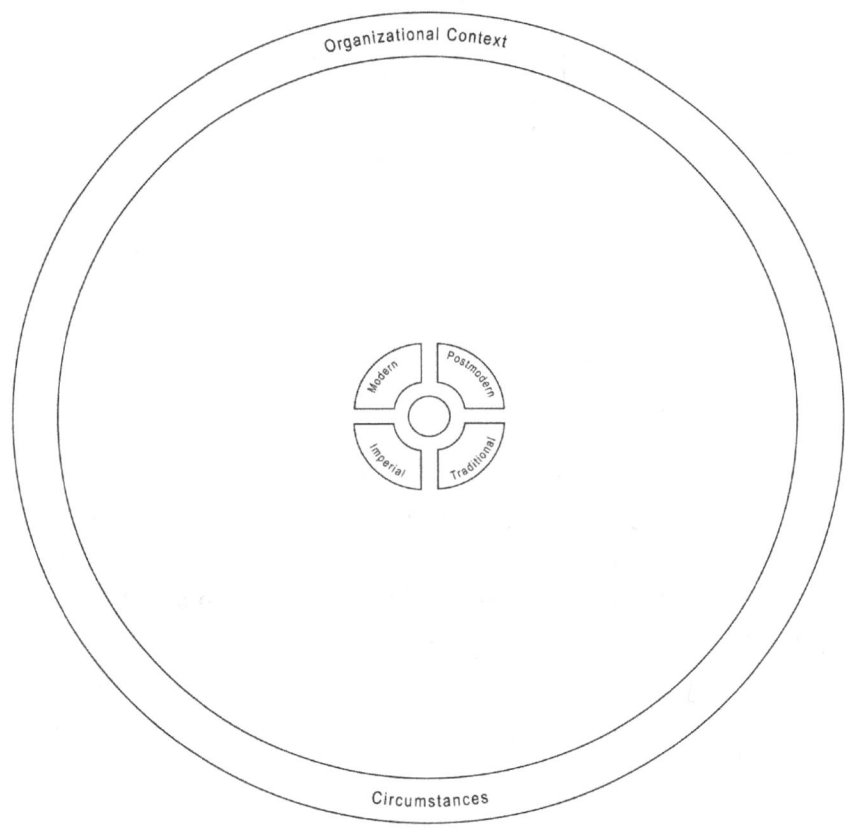

Leaders who are viewed as "credible" by followers when the leaders use the leadership style preferred by those followers (indicated in the diagram by the appropriate leadership styles being paired with follower worldviews.)

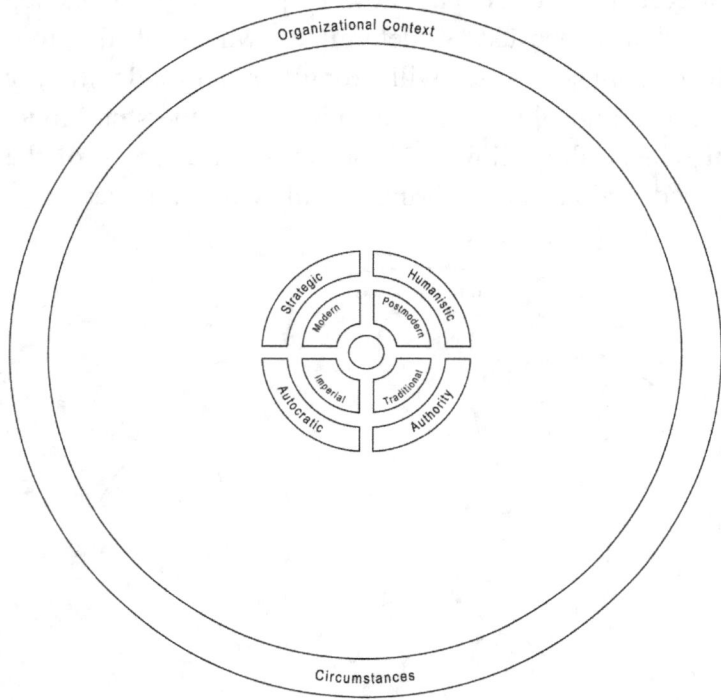

At this point, you should already know what comes next in our model. Leaders have three "inherent leadership responsibilities," also called three "essential abilities" they draw upon to fulfill their responsibilities.

The way they approach those responsibilities is a function of their "leadership style."

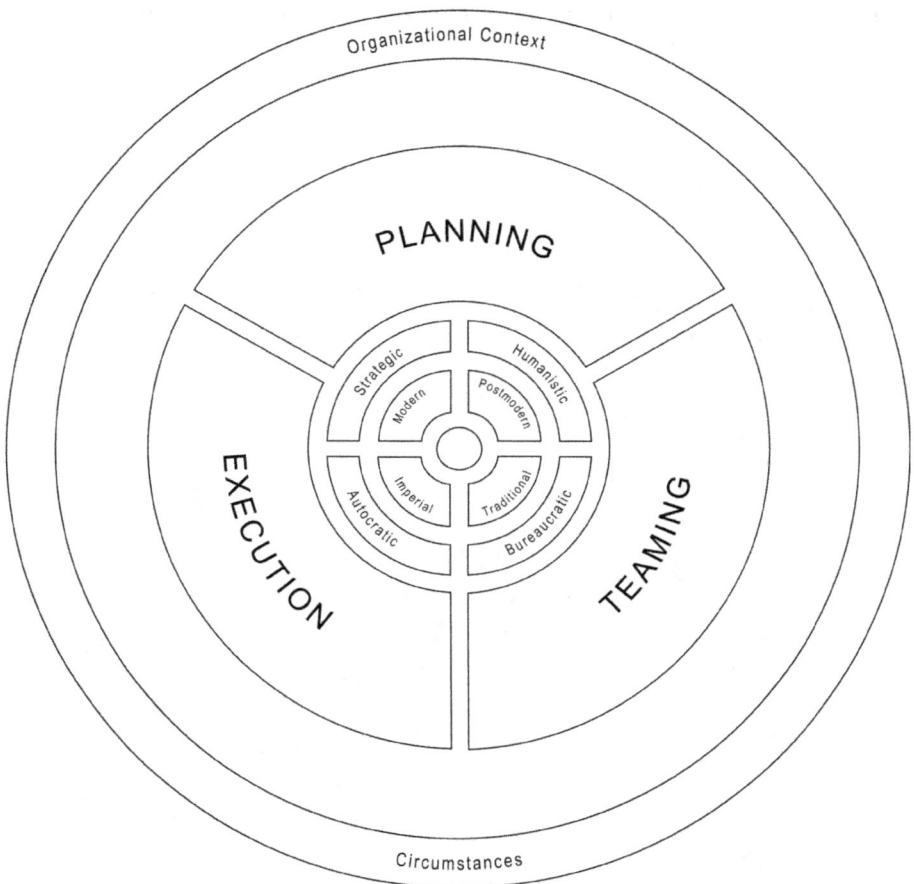

The words Planning, Teaming and Execution represent the "inherent leadership responsibilities" and also the "essential leader abilities."

Next, we know that leaders must engage in many activities, and use their "skill sets" in order to fulfill those responsibilities. Of course, each of these skill sets looks different according to the leadership style being used.

Once we bring these nine skill sets back in, we have the full Universal Leadership Model.

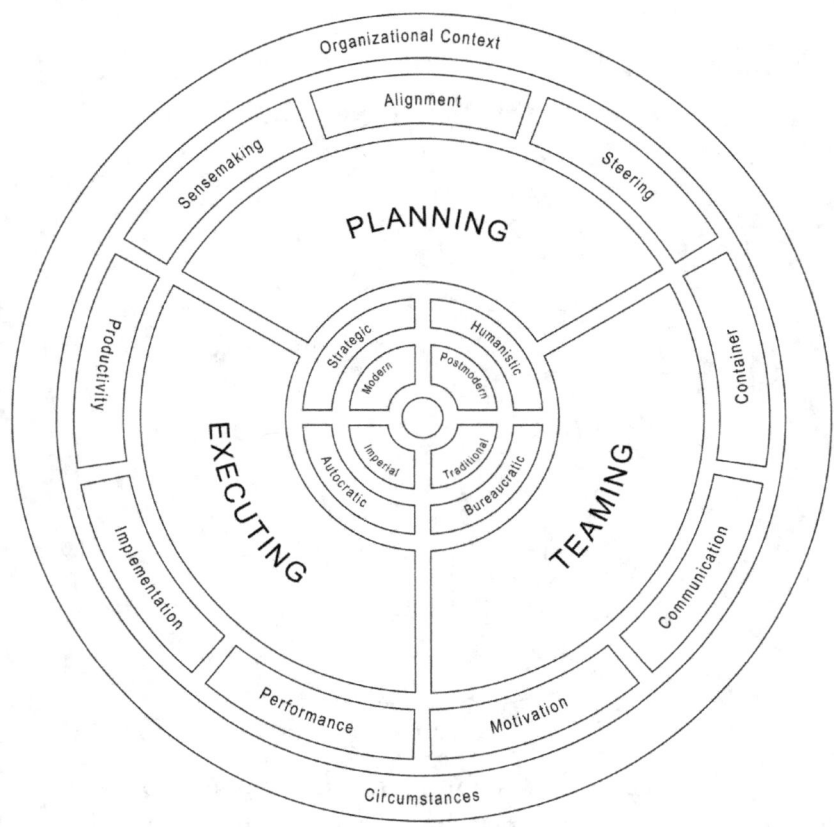

Please study this simple, yet profound, model. If you learn and apply it, it will revolutionize your leadership. This chapter provides a high-level overview of the Universal Leadership Model.

This model merits a longer discussion. If you would like to continue this discussion, with more detail and nuance, please refer to my other book, *The Universal Leadership Model: The Simplicity on the Other Side of Complexity*.

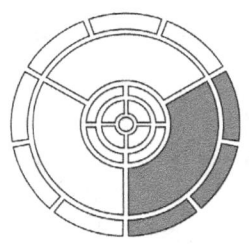

CHAPTER 4: THE ACCELERATING LEADERSHIP METHODOLOGY

Previously, I introduced the three inherent leadership responsibilities. In this chapter, I will expand upon them to unpack the most common skill sets that leaders draw upon to fulfill those responsibilities and I will introduce the world's fastest and most effective method for improving leadership performance and organizational results. In this chapter, you will be introduced to the "practice-based leadership" approach that I invented in the early 2000s at Stagen Leadership Academy and Integral Institute. As you are about to see in this chapter, this is an absolute game changer.

As mentioned in an earlier, "character traits" or vague "leadership qualities" can't be taught or learned in any reasonable amount of time. But "technique" (also known as behavior, or practices) can absolutely be trained and learned relatively quickly. This is the key to rapid leadership development.

I'm going to be blunt again here.

Please stop listening to bogus leadership advice from the leadership industry's "snake oil salesmen" who push vague concepts like EQ, confidence, trustworthiness, or charisma.

Vague concepts have never helped a leader increase this technical and complex skill. Seek advice from people who have legitimate expertise in the requisite leadership skills and "techniques" and know how to help clients develop those skills (by teaching the requisite techniques, not vague concepts).

"What, abandon EQ" you might be saying to yourself? No, of course you don't abandon your ability for emotional intelligence.

Of course emotional intelligence is important... that is the capacity that we point to when we use the term emotional intelligence is important... along with *social intelligence, cognitive intelligence, moral intelligence* and so on.

I realize these intelligences are important. In fact, I have taught and written extensively about these human capacities over the last two decades. My colleagues and I have developed assessments to measure low, medium and high levels of development along these intelligences (which integral and developmental psychologists call "lines of development").

However, and this is the key point, in my 20+ years I've never ever, not even once, seen a person's EQ improve by lecturing them about what it is.

Stop talking about emotional intelligence. You are wasting your breath and the listener's time, attention and energy.

This is a somewhat nuanced but extremely important point I am making here.

This lies at the heart of what is wrong with the leadership development industry.

> *Talking about intelligence does nothing to increase it. This is akin to taking piano lessons and the instructor talks about the qualities of great piano players. The instructor goes on and on of the benefit of "musical intelligence."*

It is so obvious when we talk about other technical and complex skills (playing a musical instrument, learning to play a sport like baseball or basketball, or learning karate).

But when we talk about the technical and complex skill of leadership, people somehow miss the obvious fact that we are talking about a technical and complex skill made up of techniques and skills.

> *If you went to basketball camp, the instructors would not talk about "athletic intelligence" (kinesthetic intelligence). Rather, you would practice dribbling, passing, shooting and rebounding!*

The only time you should be talking about intelligences or "leadership traits" is when you are creating a profile for hiring. If you are in a hiring role, then yes, you want to screen and hire people with high EQ.

This book is about leadership development.

Emotional intelligence improves when and only when you give a person a specific technique, a practice, to adopt and use daily over many months.

This is the <u>only</u> way to improve these skills: through practice.

Most leadership training and coaching programs talk about "EQ" (and trust and culture and inclusivity and so on) as vague concepts and very few offer specific techniques as daily practices that actually grow these capacities.

This is the key distinction you must grasp to appreciate this groundbreaking leadership development approach.

If your objective is to improve your leadership skills rapidly, then you will want to put most of the emphasis on the specific skill sets you need to enhance the abilities you are targeting.

We must come down out of the clouds of vague concepts into specific behaviors that can be memorized, practiced and matured with time (and with which we can layer on additional skills that comprise the complex abilities we associate with leadership).

I previously introduced three responsibilities that have always been and always will be inherent to leadership. I call these the three *Inherent Responsibilities of Leadership.*

While these three inherent responsibilities go by many names, I have been using the common terms of *planning, teaming* and *executing.*

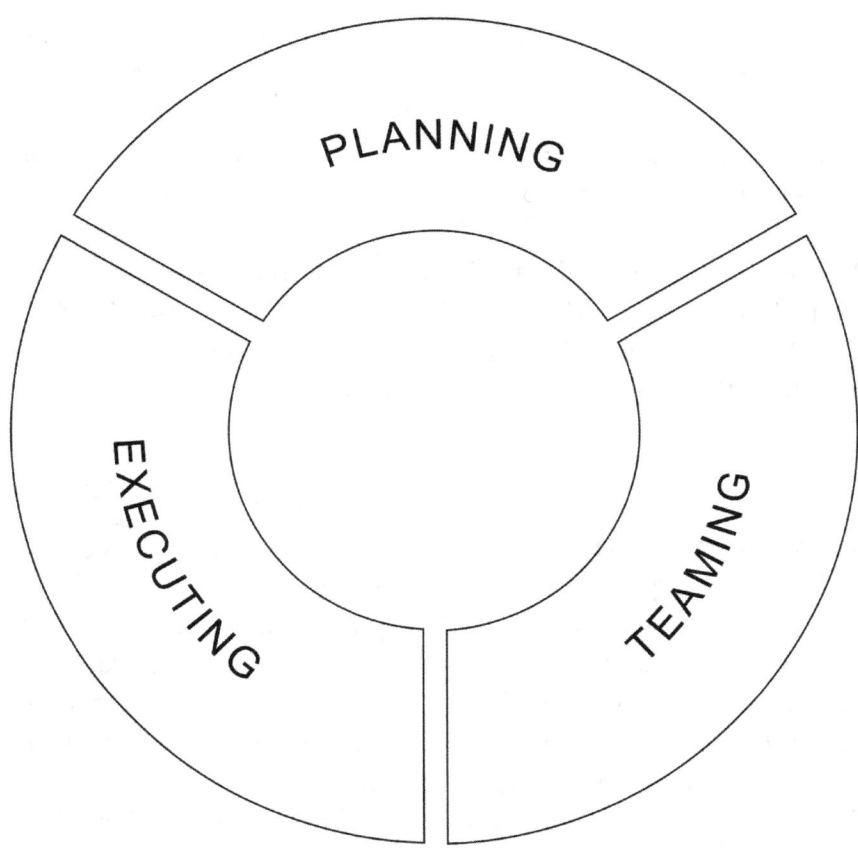

I will now begin the pivot from conventional, common ways of describing these "activities" to our more nuanced names and descriptions.

1. Planning

You will recall that leaders articulate a vision (a direction) and suggest some kind of plan to achieve that vision. They also have to align stakeholders with values and purpose of the organization and cultivate their commitment to that vision or direction, and they must guide or "steer" the organization toward that vision over time. For simplicity's sake and to feel familiar to the widest population of book readers, I've gone with the single word "planning" here, but the word "steering" would be another one-word way to describe this responsibility.

A more comprehensive and accurate title for this first dimension of leadership responsibility would be *"Strategy & Alignment."*

This is the subject of the book in this Integral Leadership series entitled: *Strategy & Alignment: How the Most Successful Leaders Analyze Organizational Needs, Create Compelling Vision, Enroll and Align Stakeholders and Craft Smart, Evolving Strategic Plans.*

2. Teaming

You will recall that leaders "create the container" and "set the tone" of the relationships among the team members. The leader establishes some kind of structure for the team(s) including the norms that people are expected to follow in terms of supporting, relating, communicating and motivating. This may be explicitly communicated or simply be implicit (setting the example that others can follow). Think of this group of activities as the interpersonal dimension of leadership. I've used the word "teaming" here, but some readers may be more resonant with the word "relating."

A more comprehensive and accurate title for this second dimension of leadership responsibility would be *"Teamwork & Culture."*

As you are aware, this is the main focus of this book you are currently reading (in this Integral Leadership series).

3. Executing

As we saw earlier, this area of leadership responsibility includes guiding productive work to execute the strategy (implement the plans), managing people's performance and the projects they are working on. It is concerned with all of the activities an organization engages in, that have to do managing projects using the appropriate tools to coordinate work across teams, meeting expectations and being able to hold each other accountable to tasks, milestones, and deadlines, and making sure that people are focused on the right things and staying productive, efficient and effective. Some people think of this as "operational leadership". You may have heard the term "boots on the ground." You might also think of this dimension as the "hands" and "feet" of leadership.

A more comprehensive and accurate title for this third dimension of leadership responsibility would be *"Execution & Performance."*

This is the subject of my other book entitled: *Execution & Performance: How the Most Successful Leaders Close Employee Performance Gaps, Maintain Accountability and High Productivity, and Consistently Deliver Exceptional Results.*

In the next section, I will pass across these three again, this time making them more comprehensive and accurate, as leadership literature would describe them, and offer a more detailed description of many of the "activities" that leaders engage in order to fulfill these responsibilities. This convention of "activities" will become extremely important.

As mentioned before, stories of great leaders and descriptions of leaders' personality traits do little (if anything) to help you become a better leader. But if you understand the activities that effective leaders do, and you learn the specific techniques (behaviors) they leverage to complete those activities successfully, then you can rapidly improve your leadership ability.

Clearly there are a lot of leadership activities that fall into these three groupings. These three abilities are comprised of skill sets, and the skill sets are, in turn, comprised of about half a dozen discrete skills (methods or techniques that have been internalized to the point that they are instinctual).

If you survey the literature on leadership, you would find dozens of discrete techniques, tactics or skills related to each of these three fundamental categories.

While there is an infinite number of techniques, methods and skills for each of these skill sets, we have found, applying Pareto's law, that it boils down to only about half a dozen specific leadership techniques / skills that matter most (for each of the nine skill sets).

This process is related to "Complex Skill Instructional Design" we discussed in the introduction chapter. This is how we learn to play baseball (throwing, catching, batting, running) or to play a musical instrument (playing notes, combining notes into chords, musical theory of keys and chord progressions, and combining these elements into songs).

> *To repeat, it is impossible to learn a complex skill (sports, martial arts, playing an instrument, flying an airplane or leadership) without breaking the complex skill down into its component parts, and then learning the technique that support each of those skills.*

Think of it this way. You and every leader you have ever worked with (or for) has drawn on these skill sets (by whatever name) to fulfill their leadership responsibilities. You may be wondering about level of skill, or level of competency. You are right to recognize that natural talent in each of these skill set areas is not evenly distributed across the population.

While all leaders engage in some version of these activities which are inherent to leadership, some are very skillful and others have not had the benefit of training and mentorship, and who may not have strong natural instincts in that area.

For example, every leader "motivates" their followers in one way or another without exception.

Similarly, even if a leader does not have any natural ability or formal training in "planning," they still make plans in some way, even if those plans are very rudimentary. Even an unsophisticated leader would say, "This is my plan."

A final example is communication. Without exception, all leaders draw upon whatever communication skills they have to coordinate efforts.

It bears repeating that these three inherent leadership responsibilities and nine skill sets are universal. Talent, training and competency level are not universal.

Some of the leaders you worked with (and for) may have been terrible at sensemaking, alignment, strategic thinking, and planning. But if they were in a leadership role for long, they were in fact doing some version of the activities that fall into that 'bucket' we call sensemaking, alignment, strategic thinking, and planning.

In my other books, I define exactly what competency looks like at lower, intermediate, and higher levels of proficiency for each of the three essential abilities and all nine core competencies. While this book on *Teamwork & Culture* details out the benchmarks in this dimension, if you want to see the benchmarks for the other two dimensions of leadership, you can find them in my other books titled *Strategy & Alignment* and *Execution & Performance* (or see the conclusion section of this book for reference of my other books).

But let's not get ahead of ourselves. For now, it is helpful to just recognize the fact that these nine skill sets are fundamental to leadership and, in turn, organizational life.

You are already doing these nine things. All leaders (who are competent enough to stay in a leadership role for very long) do some versions of these nine activities in order to fulfill their responsibilities.

To provide more nuance, rather than limit ourselves to the common and familiar way of naming and thinking about each of these nine fundamental leadership skill sets, in the next section, we will introduce new terms and descriptions.

Now, continuing with our review of the essential abilities and core competencies, we will expand beyond the familiar or common labels and introduce our own terms.

For example, "Performance" becomes "Performance Management." "Alignment" becomes "Stakeholder Alignment." "Implementation" becomes "Project Implementation." And "planning" becomes "Dynamic Steering."

We are now going through another pass across the three essential abilities which represent the three buckets of activities, and the three skill sets (core competencies of leadership) under each.

We begin with the dimension I have been referring to simply as "Planning."

Strategy & Alignment

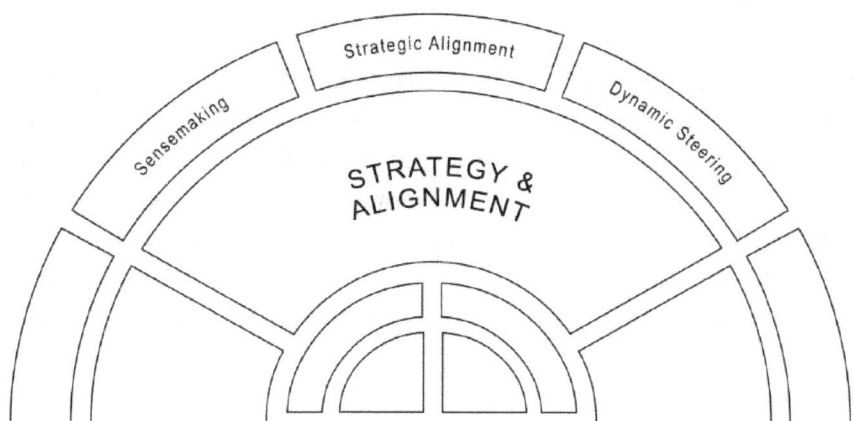

In our first pass, I called this area of responsibility simply "Planning." I will now introduce the more nuanced term, *Strategy & Alignment*.

You will recall that I defined this area of responsibility as: *establishing vision and goals, crafting strategy and plans, and enrolling stakeholder commitment.*

As we will see in this part of the book, *Strategy & Alignment* includes all of the activities related to: establishing and communicating the purpose, vision, and values of the organization, making sense of what is happening in the current environment including evaluating relevant challenges and opportunities, strategic thinking, prioritizing strategic objectives, crafting strategic plans, and enrolling stakeholder commitment in the organizational vision and the strategy to achieve shared goals.

As mentioned previously, because these skill sets are fundamental and universal, you should be able to recognize the activities in each "bucket" because they are activities that you and every other leader does in one way or another (perhaps by a different name). As we unpack each skill set in later chapters, we will weave in leadership best practices which are the behaviors that skillful leaders engage when drawing upon this skill set to fulfill their leadership responsibilities.

As the saying goes, "repetition is the mother of skill." I am sure you are aware of the benefit of revisiting and reviewing key concepts, especially, as we layer in additional distinctions. I will use this convention often in this book by re-introducing previous concepts and adding another layer of nuance. As we make a second pass over these core competencies, I will replace the simple, commonly used terms introduced previously with my more nuanced terms.

Sensemaking

This skill set is concerned with your ability to evaluate the landscape (both external conditions as well as internal organizational dynamics) to determine what is really happening, the key drivers impacting the environment, what is most important for your organization, and what is most needed.

Stakeholder Alignment

This skill set is concerned with your ability to establish and articulate your organization's direction in the form of vision, values and purpose, then to align all key stakeholders so that they feel and demonstrate a shared commitment to it.

Dynamic Steering

This skill set is concerned with your ability to develop and evolve organizational strategies, establish and revise goals and objectives, and prioritize the highest-leverage projects that will lead to desired outcomes each quarter and each year.

Teamwork & Culture

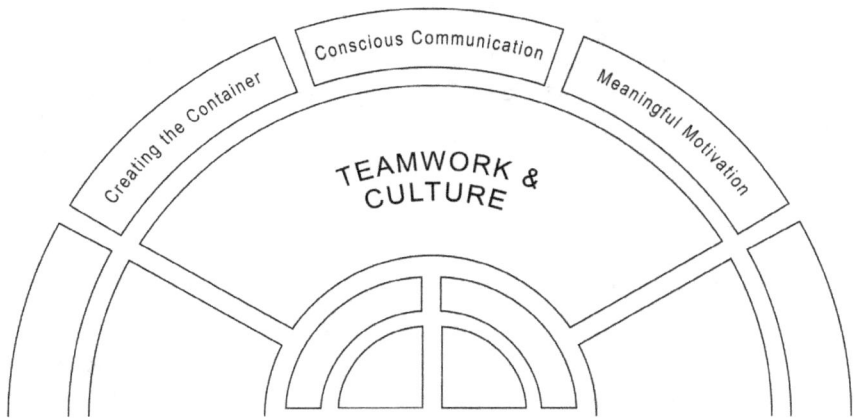

In our first pass, I called this area of responsibility and this "essential ability" simply "Teaming." I will now introduce a more nuanced term, "Teamwork & Culture."

I define this area of responsibility as: *Setting your team(s) up for success with the appropriate structure and culture, and supporting and communicating with them to keep them optimally engaged and motivated.*

Teamwork & Culture includes all of the activities related to setting your people up for success, creating and maintaining a conducive environment including a healthy culture and emotional climate, keeping people engaged and motivated using appropriate and effective communication, including feedback, listening, collaboration, and managing conflict.

Next, I will very briefly introduce each of the three skill sets that leaders draw upon to fulfill their responsibilities associated with this dimension. And I will replace the commonly-used terms, with more nuanced names.

Creating the Container

This skill set is concerned with your ability to set people up for success— this includes equipping teams with the structure, culture, training, tools and support they need to achieve shared organizational goals.

Communication

This skill set is concerned with effective communication which involves social awareness, listening, framing, feedback, dialog, collaboration, working with assumptions and interpretations, and managing conflict.

Motivation

This skill set is concerned with keeping people engaged and motivated by understanding their needs, values, and intrinsic motivators, and appealing to each person's particular worldview and leadership preferences.

Execution & Performance

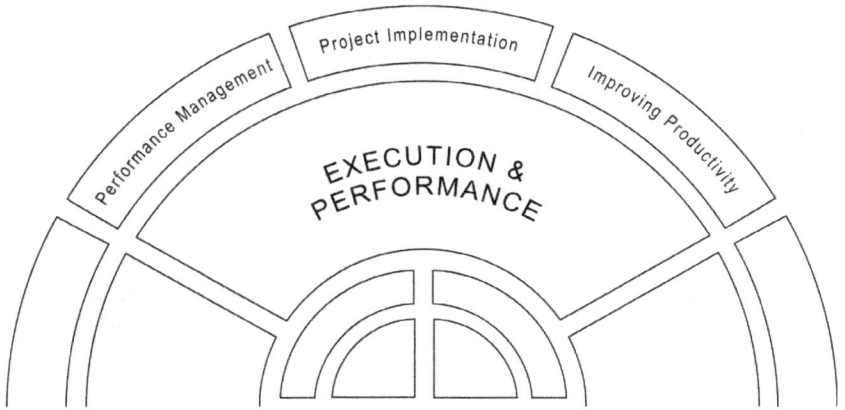

In our first pass, I called this area of responsibility and this "essential ability" simply "Executing." I will now introduce a more nuanced term, *"Execution & Performance."*

For review, I defined this area of responsibility as: *guiding productive work to execute the strategy, coordinating work, implementing projects, and managing people's performance.*

Execution & Performance, includes all of the activities related to establishing roles and responsibilities, identifying and closing performance gaps, planning and managing projects using the appropriate tools to coordinate work across teams, and maintaining high productivity so that the organizational resources are used efficiently to achieve shared goals in the desired time frames.

Performance Management

This skill set involves managing performance so that responsibilities, expectations, and agreements are consistently met, including ongoing "accountability conversations" to manage commitments and breakdowns when expectations are not met.

Implementation

This skill set is concerned with planning quarterly and monthly projects, defining objectives, workstreams, tasks and timelines, coordinating the people and activities necessary to stay on track and consistently complete projects on time and on budget.

Improving Productivity

The last skill set is concerned with your ability to help your organization complete work in a productive, organized, efficient and effective way, including managing calendars and tasks, running effective meetings, and staying focused and proactive in the face of distractions, urgencies and obstacles.

Now that we have established a high-level understanding of the nine skill sets that leaders draw upon (at whatever level of ability they currently possess) to fulfill their responsibilities, we can take bold steps toward our goal of rapidly increasing your leadership competency.

To draw again on our previously-used baseball analogy, soon we will enter the "batting cage" to work on our ability to hit the ball. But we have one more important foundation to lay that is necessary for success with an accelerating learning effort. But first, will take a close look at the four universal "follower mindsets" that unequivocally dictate which style of leadership a person will find credible, resonant and will want to follow.

Using the Right Style with the Right Followers

A person's worldview dictates how they see the world, what they believe is true about the world and the people in it, and what they value.

For leaders to be viewed as credible, they must match the correct leadership style with the followers' worldview. This is the key to all "resonant" leadership.

When a leader uses a leadership style that is associated with a worldview different from the follower's, this signals to the follower that this leader "doesn't get it." Put another way, the follower sees the leader as out of touch, clueless, not understanding what is really important, or not getting how the world really works.

A lack of "worldview alignment" results in the follower seeing the leader as not credible, not competent, or in the worst case, not trustworthy.

This is the key to what Ken Wilber and our academic colleagues call "integral leadership" which is another word for integrally-informed leadership, that is, leadership that is informed by integral psychology.

This is one of the main things that sets this leadership development approach apart from most of the other leadership learning methods available in the market.

Our approach to leadership is informed by a nuanced understanding of psychology, in particular, integral psychology which incorporates developmental psychology, worldviews and value systems, all of which are essential for effective leadership.

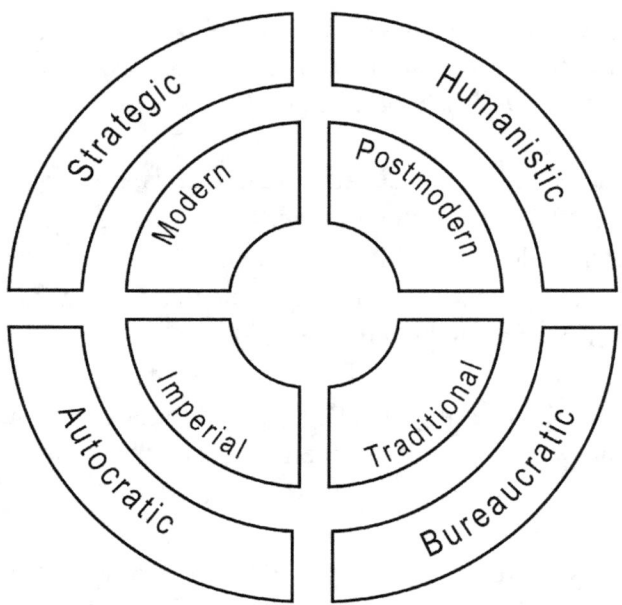

You will recall this diagram from the Universal Leadership Model that shows the four leadership styles lined up with the follower worldviews. This is absolutely essential.

As I have explained, if you use the wrong leadership style with the wrong person you run the risk of destroying your leadership credibility with that person; you will very likely appear clueless and possibly even foolish.

After teaching this unique approach to leadership to thousands of executives in corporate America, I can tell you with experience and authority that this leadership practice of "aligning leadership style with "follower mindsets" has the power to unlock and amplify the potency of the other principles and practices associated with leadership.

Using the correct "leadership style" that matches the follower's (or team's) worldview amplifies the effectiveness of every other technique described in this book and my other on leadership.

"Leadership sensemaking" is most fundamentally about "perspective taking." An integral approach to leadership involves using numerous frameworks as "lenses" which provide visibility into dimensions of reality that conventional leaders are unaware of, overlook, or ignore. The result of these superior (more accurate) lenses and precision perspective-taking practices is greater awareness, better approaches, and more skillful action.

While "matching styles with mindsets" is central to this revolutionary method, it does not represent the totality of it. Rather, it provides a logical and helpful orienting framework—like the conventions of North, South, East, West on a geographical map—to ensure that the leader is headed in the right direction. As you read this section, please be mindful of the fact that this is merely an introduction, a high-level overview of this framework. The goal is for you to become familiar with it. The application of these leadership styles (to all of the different abilities and skill sets) will come with time. It should be obvious that understanding the mindset of your followers (or your team or culture) is central to leadership effectiveness. In fact, most comprehensive leader development programs teach some methods for "understanding people."

Some simply teach listening skills, many teach various kinds of personality typology systems, and a few use stages of development (a.k.a. stages of psychological maturity) to help leaders better understand their followers and what makes them tick.

I'm going to use an American idiom—being "in the ballpark"—as an analogy to illustrate a crucial point. Those personality types, situational leadership tactics, and get-to-know-your-people methods are like finding your section and seat at a large baseball game.

Assuming that you are in the correct stadium, knowing the exact section, row and seat number is very helpful. But here's the catch. In this analogy, your followers' worldview (their values and universal beliefs) represents the stadium. If you fail to accurately recognize your followers' worldview, then you are not even in the right ballpark; therefore, the details about personality types and behavioral tendencies (even a person's goals) are essentially useless.

Worldview is the overall perspective from which one sees and interprets the world.

> *A person's worldview defines what they care about, what motivates them, what they believe is worthwhile, and what they believe lacks value or is "wrong." And as we now understand it also specifically dictates which leadership style they will be resonant with, and follow, as well as which approaches are likely to backfire.*

If you want to understand people, you first need to get "into the right ballpark" by identifying their worldview.

I believe that the failure to grasp meaning making systems—what I am calling worldviews here—lies at the heart of the problem with conventional approaches to leadership. Those approaches often wrongly assume that people's motivations are homogenous. Most conventional approaches to leadership (and also management) fail to adequately take into account the fact that people with different worldviews value different things, interpret the same facts differently, and subsequently have very different priorities. This mistake is at the heart of the "bogus leadership advice" most so-called experts offer.

Follower Mindsets Are the Key to Leadership Success

I mentioned Barbara Kellerman (author of *Bad Leadership, The End of Leadership* and *Professionalizing Leadership*) and Jeffrey Pfeffer (author of *Leadership BS)* in the introduction. Unfortunately, these two courageous "whistleblowers" are among only a few leadership experts that are acknowledging the fact that most leadership development programs focus mainly on the leader and generally ignore "context" in which the leadership is occurring. Worse, they almost all leave the followers out of the equation altogether.

Yes, you read that right. The majority of leadership training programs mostly or completely ignore the followers!

They focus the vast majority of the time talking about traits of great leaders and qualities of effective leaders with seemingly no awareness at all of the needs, worldviews and preferences of the followers. This, again, is one of the main reasons that most leadership development programs produce such criminally dismal results. In her books, Kellerman really takes the leadership industry to talk over this colossal error. She underscores the fact that any legitimate approach to leadership must take into account all three elements of the leader, the context (the circumstances), and especially the followers.

I would suggest that one of the most important aspects of a leader's context or circumstances, is their follower's worldviews. If you understand the follower's worldview (or mindset, then you will know what they care about, what is important to them, how they define leadership, and what they look for in a person they view as a credible leader.

Most importantly, if you know a person's "follower mindset," and you know how to match up the mindsets with the four Universal Leadership Styles, then you can avoid the embarrassing situation of using the wrong style with the wrong person and destroying your leadership credibility in their eyes.

In the same way that beauty is in the eye of the beholder, leadership is in the eye of the follower. If you use the wrong leadership style with the wrong person, they will not see you as a credible leader. They will see you as clueless or even foolish. A leadership approach that is extremely resonant with one employee, team or department will be ineffective or even offensive for another. The troublesome issue is: "How can you know which approach will be effective and which will be offensive?"

The answer, of course, is the follower's worldview.

As I mentioned in the section about the Leadership Rosetta Stone, integral psychology shows us that about 95% of the values/belief systems that today's leaders are likely to encounter fall into four broad worldviews.

For some readers, this fact is not new. Many readers are already familiar with Modern, Postmodern, and Traditional worldviews. However, few people are aware of the fact that these "value systems" predict with astonishing accuracy which leadership style will be resonant and appreciated, and which styles will be met with resistance and/or rejection.

It is hard to overstate the significance of this. This realization lies at the heart of the breakthrough that my team discovered, with Ken Wilber's guidance in the early 2000s. Essentially, this deceptively simple Universal Leadership Model successfully aggregates, synthesizes, and integrates, more than a 100 years of leadership theories.

Moreover, once sufficiently internalized in practice (and that takes a little time of course), this unique leadership framework allows leaders to effectively motivate and influence followers (of all kinds) with a level of precision and efficacy that is rarely witnessed.

Also, this works everywhere it has been tested. In corporate environments, financial services, construction sites, assembly lines, hospitals, police forces, military... even in remote African tribal villages.

Values Research

Worldviews are composed of values and universal beliefs. Values are perceptual filters minds use to determine ("evaluate") what is important in any given situation. Universal beliefs are broad-based beliefs about self, others, and system (how the world is perceived to work). In terms of knowing which leader a given person is likely to follow (or elect given the choice), in terms of knowing what people care about, in terms of knowing what motivates people, in terms of understanding people in the most fundamental sense, nothing is more germane than values.

The conceptualization and use of values models is widespread and informed by a multitude of different approaches that differ in details but are quite similar in principle and overarching conclusions. Values research is widely used by psychologists, political scientists, and marketers. The pervasive role of values in all aspects of human life has motivated hundreds of studies in the disciplines of psychology, sociology, cultural anthropology, and consumer behavior.

A large body of research has shown conclusively that values represent both a powerful explanation of and influence on a variety of individual and collective behaviors. In fact, in recent years, the study and measurement of values has become one of the most dynamic research areas in the social science disciplines (management, leadership, marketing and consumer behavior). Several values measurement methodologies are currently available and more are surfacing.

These worldviews, along with their correlating universal leadership styles, cut across nationalities, ethnicity, and culture. There is nothing inherently American or North American (or European or Caucasian) about these worldviews and leadership styles. However, I live in the U.S. and most of my work has involved leaders in the Americas. The examples and illustrations in my teaching reflect my experience.

Also, in this presentation, I often use the term "mindset" in place of or in addition to the more academic term "worldview."

When describing people who hold a worldview, it is often helpful to use the word "mindset" in place of the word worldview. Rather than say, this person holds a modern worldview, we could say, this person has a "modern mindset" or better still, this person has an "achiever mindset." This section of the book will follow this convention and will use "mindset" in place of "worldview." This presentation uses broad and simplified examples of single worldviews or mindsets that help new students become familiar with their basic appearance and function. Once you can begin to recognize them, in time you will begin to see how they can be combined (as some people's mindset is a blend of two such as 50/50 or 60/40).

Next, I will go through each of the four follower mindsets, describe how the world looks through that lens, refer to the massive amount of research that backs up these assertions, and give you several examples of "profiles" of employees who typify this mindset. After the explanation of the follower mindset, then I will offer a more detailed explanation of the style of leadership that should be used with people with that mindset.

Achiever Mindset

People with a modern worldview can also be described as having an "Achiever mindset." They identify with being highly rational, competitive, ambitious, autonomous and elite. They emphasize success and/or status as defined by material acquisition and "upward mobility."

They value excellence, advancement, prosperity, achievement, and status. Most importantly, they prefer to follow leaders who are perceived to have the most expertise and ability to achieve goals. In other words, they follow leaders who use the Strategic Leadership style.

The Achiever mindset (and the Strategic Leadership style) is well suited for the following environments and circumstances: sales departments, professional services firms, innovation-driven organizations, senior management positions, and in roles that require advanced levels of education such as scientific research.

Seeing the World Through an Achiever's Lens

In academic circles, this worldview is referred to as the "Modern worldview" (as contrasted to the Traditional and Postmodern worldviews).

When you look at the world through this lens, you see a playing field full of possibilities to explore and opportunities to achieve. You will emphasize the scientific and rational dimensions of what you see. The key to life is to strive for, and achieve "success."

Through this lens, it becomes easy to believe in the advancement of humankind through the application of the highly disciplined rational mind and its scientific, technological, and medical manifestations. Life is to be met and mastered by finding the best way to act on its limitless opportunities.

Empirical Research

While this worldview, or "follower mindset" may be new for a few readers, there is nothing new, novel or controversial about it; in fact, my descriptions are based on widely-accepted and respected empirical research that has come out of Harvard, Yale, Boston College, Washington University and other top institutions over the last four decades. I offer more nuanced, academic analysis in other books (especially my book series on Integral Leadership). For this introduction, I will mention the academic terms that the different leading psychologists use for this worldview / follower mindset. McClelland uses the term "Achievement," Loevinger uses "Conscientious," Kohlberg uses "Social Order," Graves uses

"Multiplistic-Achievist," Kegan uses "Institutional," Wade uses "Achievement," and Torbert uses "Achiever." When I'm using "follower mindset" terminology, I say Achiever mindset and when I'm using the worldview term, I call it the Modern worldview. Although I don't use Ken Wilber's color schemes in this book series created for mainstream readers, for my readers who are students of integral theory, I will mention here that the Wilberian color code for this worldview is "orange."

Understanding People with an Achiever Mindset

People with this mindset tend to believe that while there are many valid ways to think and behave, there is always one best way. People with this mindset want to feel they are at the "top of their game" and that they have earned (quite literally, in some cases) the recognition of belonging to an elite group.

They are not satisfied to simply "play by the rules;" rather, they want to fully understand the rules to gain a competitive advantage over those with less acuity, with the ultimate ambition of becoming so successful that they might eventually "change the rules of the game." Many of their decisions will be motivated by the promise of success and status, as well as an awareness and fairly sophisticated understanding of the dynamics of the overall system within which they operate (company, church, nation, global marketplace).

Some examples of occupational roles that tend to epitomize the Achiever mindset include salespeople, attorneys, research scientists, marketing agents, PR and advertising representatives, elected public officials, architects, and physicians in conventional practice (as opposed to alternative medicine which would very likely be someone with a Pluralistic mindset described in the next section). Following are some example profiles of people with these mindsets.

Rob - Research Scientist

I'm a research scientist who's convinced that most of the world's problems can be solved with the right technological advancements and tools. I think that many people hold superstitious, irrational beliefs that are detrimental to society's interests and retard scientific progress. While I enjoy my work during the week, I pursue my real passion on the weekends. I've completed over twenty triathlons and placed in the top five in most of them. My training schedule could probably qualify as some sort of third world form of punishment, but when I cross the finish line in first place it's all worth it. There's a force in me that's relentless in its determination to win. There's something exhilarating about testing your limits and pushing your personal edge.

Danielle - Attorney

I just graduated from Harvard Law School and I am joining one of the most prestigious firms in the country. I grew up in a two-parent working class household and was a latch-key kid. My parents were focused on providing necessities for us. They helped me to see that hard work and determination are keys to success. While I respect my parents "traditional" ways, I knew from a young age that I wanted to work smarter, not harder, to enjoy the finer things in life. And while my parents' religious orientation works for them, I wasn't satisfied with simplistic answers to complex questions. To be honest, I believe that the world would be a better place if more people would put their faith in reason and look to science rather than religion for answers.

Lee - Small Business Owner

I own a small web-based company that produces and sells custom laptop cases for the fashion-conscious consumer. As a start-up, I wasn't entirely sure what I was doing but decided to take some calculated risks while telling myself that failing wasn't an option. I became incredibly focused and goal-oriented, and within two years I was featured as Entrepreneur of the Year in a nation-wide magazine.

Strategic Leadership is Strongly Preferred

People like Lee, Danielle and Rob who have an Achiever worldview prefer to follow leaders who embody personal excellence and success and who are perceived to be most likely to achieve predefined goals.

In this form of leadership, the person with the most expertise leads via strategic planning and tangible incentives. It is characterized by incentivizing teams to execute well-conceived plans to outperform their competitors. In academic terms, this approach is sometimes referred to as "transactional" to differentiate it from the "transformational" quality of the Collaborative Leadership style.

It's easy to see how the Achiever mindset finds this strategic, goal-oriented leadership approach resonant.

In fact, as we shall see, the developers and advocates of the many "schools of leadership" that fall into this category nearly always possess the corresponding worldview.

This explains why academics / researchers / authors who are enthusiastic proponents of each leadership style believe that their style is the best and should be used in every situation.

When you are with a group of people who share the same values system, if you pay attention to their language, you will notice that they have a way of communicating with each other that reflects their common values and beliefs.

My mentor Ken Wilber refers to this as the "Dominant Mode of Discourse." I use the shorter term "Values Dialect" (or simply dialect). This values dialect is the dialect of business.

Leaders whose primary mindset is Affiliative or Traditional who want to be taken seriously in business need to learn to speak the Achiever dialect even if it is not their "native tongue."

Affiliative Mindset

People with an affiliative mindset identify with being nonjudgmental, egalitarian, and socially and environmentally conscious.

They value connection, tolerance, cultural sensitivity, diversity, sustainability, and interdependence. They strive for fulfillment as defined by personal growth, increased awareness, harmonious relationships, and "making a difference."

Most importantly, they prefer to follow leaders who are perceived as being aware, sensitive to the wellbeing of others, value consensus, and always treat others as equals; in other words, leaders who use a Humanistic leadership style. My colleagues and I also refer to this style as the "Collaborative" leadership style. I will use both terms in this book series.

Seeing the World Through an Affiliative Lens

In academic circles, this worldview is referred to as the "Postmodern Worldview" (as opposed to the Modern or Traditional). It is sometimes also called a "pluralistic" worldview.

Sociologist and bestselling author Paul Ray uses the term "Cultural Creatives" to describe people who identify with the worldview. In his book *The Cultural Creatives: How 50 Million People Are Changing the World*, he summarizes research on 50 million adult Americans (slightly over one quarter of the adult population). Ray presents a significant amount of demographic and psychographic research comparing and contrasting this worldview to the Traditional worldview and Modern worldview.

When you look at the world through this Postmodern or "pluralistic" lens, you see a diverse ecosystem where cooperation leads to synergy.

The dictionary definition of pluralistic is: "a social perspective that believes no single explanatory system or view of reality can account for all the phenomena of life; rather there are many (plural) truths. Further, it is desirable to have numerous distinct ethnic, religious, or cultural groups present and tolerated in society."

Empirical Research

My descriptions in this book are all based on empirical research out of Harvard, Yale, Boston College, Washington University and other top institutions over the last four decades. For this introduction, I will mention the academic terms that the different leading psychologists use for this worldview / follower mindset. McClelland uses the term "Affiliative," Loevinger uses "Individualistic," Kohlberg uses "Social Contract," Graves uses "Relativistic-Personalistic," Kegan uses "late-institutional" into "early-Interindividual," Wade uses "Affiliative," and Torbert uses "Individualist." Although I don't use Ken Wilber's color schemes in this book series created for mainstream readers, for my readers who are students of integral theory, I will mention here that the Wilberian color code for this worldview is "green."

Understanding People with an Affiliative Mindset

Historically, leaders with the postmodern worldview and Affiliative mindset were responsible for the human rights and environmental movements.

People with this mindset tend to display egalitarian, tolerant attitudes, and are often enthusiastic endorsers of equal rights and equal opportunity for all people in all situations. People with this mindset want to feel as though they are "making a difference."

Their decisions tend to be motivated by the belief that their choice will help them (or their organization) continue to grow and develop, and that the world will be positively impacted (or at least not negatively affected) by their actions.

Whereas, people with the Achiever mindset emphasize external/material accomplishments (financial success, material acquisitions, status), people with this Affiliative mindset prefer to emphasize internal/intangible accomplishments (awareness, human connection, emotional fulfillment).

As such, they are more motivated by personal growth, people, and relationships than by material gain.

Of course this group can be highly motivated to achieve material success for a social or environmental cause as long as this is accomplished without sacrifices of personal growth or rewarding relationships.

People with this mindset gravitate toward communities that value tolerance for multiple perspectives, interdependence, creativity, diversity, activism, and "progressive" approaches.

They prefer nontraditional, "humanized" workplaces where self-expression is encouraged and rewarded; where contribution to social, political, and environmental causes is mission-critical or intrinsic to profitability; where duties and roles are actively interchanged in the service of a nonhierarchical, egalitarian approach; where team and roundtable gatherings are standard to internal operations and decision-making; where the job requires higher education; and where ongoing growth and development along with "work-life-balance" are encouraged. Following, I provide some profiles of people with this Affiliative mindset. I am certain one of these profiles (if not more than one) will remind you of someone you know. Pay attention to these patterns, they are all around you, and the sooner you begin to recognize them, the sooner you will know which leadership style or approach will be resonant with them.

Jonathan - Volunteer

Right out of college I joined the Peace Corps. At some point during my senior year, I realized that most of the world's population will never have the opportunities I once took for granted. Today, I work as a diversity consultant in the public sector, I help people within organizations accept and find strength in each others' differences. There's a real tendency in all of us to feel that our own way of looking at things is intrinsically superior, and it's this attitude that is responsible for most of the world's conflict. If everyone would accept each other's differences, we'd finally have a peaceful planet.

Delia - Record Label Owner

At eighteen, I founded my own music label because I wanted to promote social justice and retain artistic integrity that a corporate mentality wouldn't allow. After selling over 50,000 of my albums, the major labels came courting with huge deals. Because they wanted me to compromise, I declined. Today, my label is an internationally known icon for independent art, political action, and grassroots sponsorship.

Larry - Physician

I'm an MD and the founder of a holistic health care company that's committed to people and the planet first and profit second. I've taken great care to give everyone in my organization an equal voice; there is no hierarchy to speak of, and decision-making is done by consensus. As far as I'm concerned, a good business should function a lot like a democracy to ensure that too much power isn't invested in any one person. It's clear to me that the modern lifestyle being commercialized and relentlessly promoted by megacorporations is environmentally unsustainable for the planet. When I recognized I was part of the problem, I decided to become part of the solution by simplifying my life and limiting my consumption.

Humanistic Leadership is Strongly Preferred

People like Larry, Delia and Jonathon who have an Affiliative mindset prefer to follow leaders who are perceived as being aware, sensitive to the wellbeing of others, value consensus, and treat others as equals. People with the Affiliative mindset believe that leadership is not vested in any single person; rather, it should be consensus-based in the sense that self-managed teams should lead themselves.

This approach is considered "transformational" and involves inviting people's perceptions, feelings and intuition via roundtable discussion and dialog to arrive at consensus, then work collaboratively toward common goals that serve the greater good. It is also called "Collaborative" leadership. Leadership is also likely to be understood as situational and temporary; nearly all position-based authority is therefore highly questionable or even rejected outright. Unlike the Traditional mindset, people with the Affiliative mindset abhor hierarchy and will tend to either ignore it or seek to actively undermine it.

Many of the books that promote work-life balance, emotionally-aware "resonant" leadership, and "appreciative inquiry" are both popular with people having a Affiliative mindset and were written by people with Affiliative mindsets. Katzenbach and Smith's bestselling book, *The Wisdom of Teams,* was mentioned earlier in the leadership theory section of this book.

When authors are subject to their own worldview (and fail to recognize the different worldviews at play in the workplace), they tend to advocate their approach as the best approach. This is another example of the rampant unconscious worldview bias that we see in this field of leadership development.

In fact, it is Humanistic leadership (also called "transformational leadership" or "collaborative leadership") that is currently in the vanguard of popular business literature. For many leaders, this humanistic, transformational approach is a welcome shift away from the transactional and traditional (Authority) approaches that have been popular for so long. However, sophisticated leaders see the flaw in this thinking. There is no best leadership approach for all types of people. The best leadership approach is the one that will be most resonant with the people you hope to lead.

Humanistic leadership works great with people with Affiliative mindsets. However, people with an Achiever mindset consider it to be too touchy-feely, people with a Traditional mindset consider its relativistic values to be immoral, and people with a Power mindset interpret kindness and sensitivity as weaknesses and steamroll right over it.

Traditional Mindset

People with a Traditional Mindset identify with being responsible, purposeful, and self-sacrificing. They seek a reassuring sense of stability, security, and belonging by conforming to a worldview that they unambiguously describe as the tried and true "natural order of things."

This natural order of things is defined by the long-standing traditions of the culture in which they were socialized. As you would expect, people with this mindset prefer to follow leaders who are perceived as having positional and/or moral authority; in other words, leaders who use an Authoritarian Leadership style.

Seeing the World Through a Traditional Lens

You no doubt recognize that this is what academics refer to as the "Traditional worldview" (contrasting it with the familiar Modern and Postmodern Worldviews).

When you look through this Traditional lens, you see an ordered existence under the control of a higher authority and ultimate Truth.

Although amber is the integral theory color code we associate with this worldview, when you look through the lens, what you actually see is black-and-white.

People who use this lens to view the world perceive a concrete, literal, dualistic world of right and wrong, insiders and outsiders, believers and non-believers, and good and evil. They also see people who conform to rigid traditional roles (such as man earning money and women staying home and raising children) as following the "natural order of things" and people who deviate from conventional roles (such as people who are gender fluid, non-binary or identify as trans) as aberration at best and evil at worst.

If you know what to look for it is very easy to spot people with this Traditional mindset.

Empirical Research

My descriptions are all based on empirical research from Harvard, Yale, Boston College, Washington University and other top institutions over the last four decades. For this introduction, I will mention the academic terms that the different leading psychologists use for this worldview / follower mindset. McClelland uses the term "Authority," Loevinger uses "Conformist," Kohlberg uses "Interpersonal Accord" and "Conformity," Graves uses "Absolutistic-Obedience," Kegan uses "Interpersonal," Wade uses "Conformist," and Torbert uses "Diplomat."

When I'm using "follower mindset" terminology, I say Traditional mindset and Traditional worldview. Although I don't use Ken Wilber's color schemes in this book series created for mainstream readers, for my readers who are students of integral theory, I will mention here that the Wilberian color code for this worldview is "amber." Also some readers may be familiar with the National Values Center / Spiral Dynamics colors, which is "blue" for this mindset.

Understanding People with a Traditional Mindset

People with Traditional mindsets tend to be dedicated, reliable, loyal, responsible, conscientious, and can be expected to think and act in routine, predictable ways.

They are oriented around learning and following the rules defined by authority, and are more than willing to subjugate their own impulses and desires in the service of a greater calling, cause, or mission that they find meaningful, purposeful and in accord with their traditional beliefs.

While "Blue Collar jobs" are typical, people with this mindset are especially attracted to work that promotes what they consider to be the moral good (e.g., ministers, teachers, police officers, guidance counselors, children's athletic coaches, etc.). In addition to preferring jobs that require routine and discipline, this group thrives in circumstances that others might view as repetitive or tedious. Consequently, they excel in standards and compliance roles as well as organizational and system maintenance jobs.

People with this Traditional mindset value hierarchy; therefore, they respond best to clearly defined rules, deadlines, responsibilities and a well-defined chain of command. They also appreciate a written code of conduct to refer to, especially one that offers clear protocols for action and predictable consequences for success and failure.

Wherever in the world you encounter the Traditional worldview, it will define acceptable and unacceptable gender roles, sexual orientations and practices, food and drink consumption, and of course spiritual practices based on the long-standing traditions endemic to the culture they were raised in.

For people with this Traditional mindset, there is one and only one right way to think and behave. Conforming to authority's prescribed "right" way to think and behave is the key to ensure future rewards.

It is very important to understand that while the details of the local customs and culture (including religious practices) will differ, the broad-based core values and universal beliefs that comprise a Traditional worldview will be identical anywhere on the planet, whether it be Tehran, Turkey, Thailand or West Texas.

As an integrally-informed leader, you must understand that in Traditional cultures, both Modern and Postmodern values tend to be viewed not only with skepticism and suspicion, but often with fear and in some cases, hatred.

Fear is a major motivator underlying a feeling of "us vs. them" in the form of a common enemy that threatens the traditional way of life of the traditional lifestyle.

Proponents of the Traditional worldview (regardless of country or culture) understand these drives inherently and use positional or perceived moral authority to galvanize loyalty and motivate followers (or perhaps to gain views and viewers or sell books).

In the U.S., books such as Sean Hannity's *Deliver Us from Evil* and Bill O'Reilly's *Culture Warrior* make a convincing case that Modern and Postmodern values are a dangerous threat to the traditional way of life. So do Ann Coulter's books and Tucker Carlson's talk show episodes. These are all good examples of this fear and hatred of worldviews that deviate from the traditional view and traditional lifestyle.

The traditional mindset is based on a "parental orientation" to reality that is binary, there are parents and children and not much in between.

The leader is a parental figure and the followers are like children who should obey. The leader is seen as the authority. This is why in leadership theory, it is referred to as "authoritarian" leadership. For the traditional mindset, the authority (who is in the position of parent) should tell the followers (who are in the position of children) how to work, succeed, be moral, and generally live a good life (according to God's plan or according to the "one true way").

To an individual who holds this Traditional worldview, the person that has been annointed, appointed or elected is the de facto leader.

People with a traditional mindset view leadership as "positional." So the "Minister" and the "Mayor" are the defacto leaders.

There is one very important exception to this principle.

If the appointed or elected person does not share their traditional values and beliefs, then they will be rejected. This is very important to understand.

In this scenario, the elected leader is viewed as *illegitimate, a fake, a fraud*, or an *opportunist* who is only doing it for egocentric gain, and should be removed from that position as quickly as possible, in some cases, by any means necessary!

This reliably explains and predicts the right-wing behavior toward elected leaders viewed as "liberals."

Perhaps there is no better example of this than how the United States traditional values voters reacted to the election of Barack Obama. They (with rare exceptions) despised him, because they fear and often hate leaders that do not share their traditional values and beliefs. We saw this again when Joe Biden was elected as U.S. president.

Note that I said "that they believe" follow their traditional values. Unfortunately, it is not difficult for actual opportunists (a.k.a. "autocrats") who do not actually have traditional beliefs to convince gullible traditional voters that they do share their traditional beliefs in order to win their support or their votes.

This is why it is very common for traditional voters to vote against their own best interests and to elect politicians who are actually just manipulating them.

Following, I will share some profiles of stereotypical traditional mindset followers. I'm sure you will recognize one or all three of these profiles as employees, colleagues, or perhaps members of your family. Try to look for those patterns.

Once you learn to recognize these mindsets in others, you will know exactly which of the four universal leadership styles they will find resonant, will trust and will willingly follow and for whom they will offer their discretionary effort.

Recall earlier, I said that if you use the wrong leadership style with the wrong follower, they will not see you as credible, worse, they may see you as clueless or even foolish.

Here is a real-life example of that principle in action.

If you use a Humanistic leadership style (a.k.a. collaborative, transformational or "self-managed teams") with one of these people, it will destroy your credibility in their eyes. They will see you as just "not getting it" (that is you don't get how the world really is). And they may see you as clueless, or even foolish.

So as you read about John, Susan and Daniel on the following pages, use this opportunity to find your followers in these descriptions!

John - True Believer

It's true, I've been called "straight laced" more than once. But people who know the Truth have a duty to defend it, even if it means being politically incorrect. People talk about "shades of gray" but as far as I'm concerned, right is right and wrong is wrong. Ultimately, almost everything is black and white, and those who suggest otherwise are just avoiding moral responsibility.

Susan - School Counselor

I love God, my family, and my country—in that order. I'm particularly proud of my nationality—when I hear people criticizing the leaders of my country I tend to feel rather insulted and often angry. I really feel that some things are simply not ours to question, and that obedience and loyalty are the highest virtues to which a person can aspire for. I work as a school counselor. I'm sometimes baffled why so many of today's kids go to such great lengths to be "different." By striving to be such "non-conformists" they don't fit in. Also, I feel frustrated by our school's tolerance for modes of dress and conduct that I find socially unacceptable and are against the family values that all schools should reinforce.

Daniel - Faith-Based Counselor

I teach a vocational rehab class for single parents and one of the things I stress to my students is that if you follow the rules—both in my class and life in general—you're bound to come out all right. With the world as unpredictable as it is, it just doesn't pay to take many risks or deviate from what's been proven to work. What is most important is having stability and knowing that you and those you love will have a secure future.

Authority Leadership is Strongly Preferred

People like John, Susan and Daniel who have a Traditional worldview prefer to follow leaders they perceive as having positional or moral authority, who share their traditional beliefs, and who lead using strict adherence to a "chain of command" or the "rules" of the institution that has bestowed that authority. In other words, people with traditional mindsets see the "Authority" leader (also called "Authoritarian" leader) as the most credible, legitimate and trustworthy leaders.

This term, "authoritarian leadership," is, in fact, the well-researched, widely- acknowledged and accurate academic term for this authority-centric style of leadership.

For corporate audiences, especially ones that are composed of a lot of traditionalists, the term "Authority leadership" is preferred.

In this leadership style, the person with *positional authority* leads via chain of command. This approach is "Hierarchical" and is characterized by compliance with the rules to meet the requirements dictated by the person with authority.

While fear and guilt are primary motivators for people with a Traditional mindset, they do not want their leaders to show either of these emotions. Effective Authority leaders intuit this and rarely, if ever, admit they don't know something or admit when they have made a mistake, or admit they are afraid.

That kind of "vulnerability based self-disclosure works will Humanistic leadership with followers with an Affiliative mindset, but Authoritarity leaders (with Traditional followers) rarely if ever admit their mistakes, their lack of knowledge or their fears, doubts or uncertainties.

George W. Bush, a well-known authoritarian leader, understood this implicitly as he is having a "Traditional" mindset and his native style is Authority. In his eight years as President of the United States, even in the face of incontrovertible evidence of poor judgment and costly errors (financial, military, international affairs, many millions of unnecessary deaths and so on), he never admitted making mistakes.

While many have criticized this behavior, to his credit, this was exactly what his large base of "traditional values voters" wanted to see in their leader.

People with other mindsets tend to view this trait as an inability to admit mistakes or learn from them, yet people with this Traditional mindset will describe this same behavior as "principled."

Using the same Traditional lens, popular leadership authors and theorists (including many "leadership experts") write books about the innate "character traits of leaders," the enduring "laws of leadership," or the "steps to being a great leader."

Author John Maxwell's bestselling books are excellent examples of the traditional view of leadership.

While Modern and Postmodern writers criticize what they consider to be reductionist approaches to life and leadership, it is very important to remember that advocates of this worldview (such Tucker Carlson, Glenn Beck, Sean Hannity, Ann Coulter) are so popular precisely because a large percentage of the population (estimated 40% in the U.S.) have adopted this Traditional worldview.

Integrally-informed leadership is concerned with seeing the world as it actually is and meeting people in it as they actually are. Integrally-informed leaders realize that although the Authority leadership style may lack a certain nuance as compared to other styles, it is exactly the approach that a very large percentage of the population is most resonant with.

Power Mindset

Previously, I used the word "Imperial" to describe this worldview. As mentioned previously, worldviews are a psychological and somewhat academic term. For corporate audiences, we often pivot to "mindset" terminologies to offer a more user-friendly vernacular.

Here, when describing people who hold this worldview, I will introduce a new term, the "Power-Centric Mindset" or "Power Mindset" for short.

People with a Power mindset identify with being strong, courageous risk takers, who are capable of defending themselves in a dangerous world and getting what they want, when they want it.

They emphasize personal power as defined by the ability to live outside conventional rules and gratify their desires. They value power, protection, freedom, respect, and control. Most importantly, they prefer to follow leaders who are perceived as being the strongest, toughest, and most dominant; in other words, leaders who use an Autocratic Leadership style.

Seeing the World Through a Power-Centric Lens

Academics refer to this worldview as the "Imperial worldview". It's easy to see this worldview dominating many periods of human history. You have probably heard it described as "Machiavellian."

This term derives from the book The Prince written in 1513 by Niccolo Machiavelli as a pragmatic guide to getting and keeping power in a dangerous world. In The Prince, Machiavelli famously advocates "the ends justify the means." This pretty much sums up the Imperial worldview and the Autocratic Leadership style that is best paired with it.

When you look at the world through this Power-centric lens, you see a jungle filled with predators and self-centered people, where only the strongest and most cunning survive and thrive.

If this is your world, or at least your worldview, you tend to view others as competitors for scarce resources and will tend to interpret hesitation, softness, or even kindness, as signs of weakness.

From this point of view, team members are useful allies in the on-going quest for power and when a common enemy is identified, the team can marshal its resources quite effectively.

To this worldview, "might" really does make "right."

The "haves" deserve their status and privilege because they are powerful and dominant, and the "have not's" deserve their status because of their weakness or incompetence. Above all, people with the Power mindset value power and respect, and will respond favorably only to leaders who are perceived to be powerful and who "command respect."

Empirical Research

My descriptions in this book are all based on empirical research out of Harvard, Yale, Boston College, Washington University and other top institutions. For this introduction, I will mention the academic terms that the different leading psychologists use for this worldview / follower mindset. McClelland uses the term "Power," Loevinger uses "Self-Protective," Kohlberg uses "Self-Interest," Graves uses "Egocentric-Exploitive," Kegan uses "Imperial," Wade uses "Egocentric," and Torbert uses "Opportunist."

When I'm using "follower mindset" terminology, I say Power mindset and when I'm using the worldview term, I call it the Imperial worldview. Although I don't use Ken Wilber's color schemes in this book series created for mainstream readers, for my readers who are students of integral theory, I will mention here that the Wilberian color code for this worldview is "red."

Understanding People with a Power Mindset

People who identify with the Power mindset tend to be persuasive, egocentric, courageous, impulsive, and often charismatic. People with this mindset play crucial roles in society: the need for people who possess great courage and inner strength, and are willing to take enormous risks. However, people with this mindset are not always appreciated, because they also tend to be fiercely independent—"I live by my rules alone" and are disinterested in conforming to the status quo (including many societal norms). They have a tendency to think mainly of themselves and can be insensitive to others' needs and desires in their own uncompromising push to break free from limits, satisfy their desires, or impose their will.

Although both the Power and Achiever mindsets are driven to "win" or "dominate", the "Achiever" drive is fueled by excellence / competitiveness / status while the Power mindset is motivated by power / respect / glory. The Imperial worldview and this Power mindset can be found in every socioeconomic system, but may be more readily noticeable in inner cities and in isolated rural areas.

It is common to encounter people with this mindset in tough environments such as reform schools, heavy construction, oil and gas refineries, and prisons. These are the life conditions that give rise to and reward Power mindsets. Oftentimes people with a Power mindset were raised in or spent many years in these life conditions. When they move on to new circumstances they may carry that worldview with them. As you would expect, people with this mindset gravitate toward social groups that value toughness, aggression, and physical prowess and that encourage behavior sometimes considered "beneath social norms."

Following are profiles of people with a Power mindset. As with the other profiles I have provided in this book, please use these as archetypes and think about how these profiles remind you of some of the people in your life, or perhaps former bosses or co-workers.

People with this Power mindset do not respond well to "Strategic" leadership, to "Collaborative" (or "Humanistic") leadership, or to the parental "Authority" style of leadership. Followers with this mindset only respect Autocratic leadership. So, it is important that you recognize this mindset by seeing the patterns that I am providing you in these profiles.

Mike - Bouncer

I grew up in a tougher part of town—maybe that explains why I've always felt most comfortable in situations where it's "do or die." I did well in school but was bored with it. I dropped out of college and worked as a bouncer for a few years. I enjoyed it but I wanted to make money, so I parlayed my intellect, instinct, and charisma into a successful career in mergers and acquisitions. It's a ruthless business well-suited for me—I was never shy about drawing blood. I work hard and play hard. I generally stay out of trouble though I have had a few close calls. Ask my friends and they'll tell you there's never a dull moment.

Jill - Conservative Talk Radio Host

I've hosted my own radio show for about five years now. It's a tough gig, but fortunately, I enjoy a game of hardball. Though I'm charismatic, I'm known for going for the jugular and being able to verbally dominate a caller, even if their argument is better than mine. Basically, I operate on the premise that if somebody's not strong enough to hold their own with me, they don't deserve much respect.

Sheila - Server

I learned a long time ago that power leads to getting what you want, and that a woman with sex appeal has power over most men. Today, I'm a waitress in one of the most exclusive clubs in town. I basically make a killing by pouring on the nice and, when necessary, flashing a bit of skin. But it's not just about the money, I like the feeling that I'm in control. And I like working in an atmosphere where people aren't concerned about anything but having a good time.

Autocratic Leadership is Strongly Preferred

People like Sheila, Mike and Jill with this Power-centric mindset only willingly follow leaders who they respect, and they do not respect weakness.

Therefore, they tend to follow leaders who are perceived as having the most power, in other words, leaders who use an Autocratic Leadership style. Power-centric followers are motivated by power and respect, not by "people skills."

The Autocratic approach to leadership is "Unilateral" and can be summed up as follows: *impose one's will through reputation, fear and respect, tightly control information and choices, reward compliance and punish disloyalty.*

Try to recall how the world appears through the lens of an Imperial worldview.

If you perceive the world as a jungle or battlefield, then you are likely to believe the best way to advance toward your goals is always to protect yourself, gain power, and outmaneuver others who are perceived as either obedient loyalists or as obstacles, enemies or threats. Note that for autocratic leaders, both the obedient loyalists and the enemies are seen as objects to be manipulated.

If you read any of the numerous books written by former Donald Trump employees (about the man's leadership style) you will discover a textbook-accurate description of this Autocratic leadership approach.

As mentioned in an earlier chapter, bookstores are filled with popular titles that advocate this Autocratic leadership style. As I mentioned, these numerous books would not be so popular if there wasn't a market for them. I will remind you of the Stanly Bing books: *What Would Machiavelli Do? The Ends Justify the Meanness* and *Sun Tzu Was a Sissy: Conquer Your Enemies, Promote Your Friends, and Wage the Real Art of War* and the Robert Greene books *The 48 Laws of Power* and *The 50th Law*. Greene writes, "Learning the game of power requires a certain way of looking at the world, a shifting of perspective." From this autocratic perspective, everyone wants power and everyone is in a constant duplicitous game to gain more power at the expense of others.

While this autocratic style can be extremely useful on the battlefield or the oil field, unfortunately, this style has been seen on the rise even in modern countries, even in prominent leadership roles in government.

Many books (and studies) are available that provide a detailed account of the advantages and (huge) disadvantages seen when this style of leadership is deployed outside of the battlefield or oil field. Much carnage ensues.

Another excellent resource for students of Autocratic leadership, especially when it is used in the wrong context, see Harvard's Barbara Kellerman's book, *The Enablers: How Team Trump Flunked the Pandemic and Failed America*. The problem with this autocratic leadership approach is that people for whom the autocratic leadership style is their dominant style tend to be primarily or exclusively concerned with themselves and perhaps their immediate family or shareholders. Autocratic leadership simply does not work very well when those leaders have the responsibility of the wellbeing of a large diverse constituency of people whose welfare rely on wise decision-making that benefits the greater good.

However, we must never lose sight of the fact that people with a Power mindset, like Mike, Sheila and Jill in our profile examples, strongly prefer autocratic leaders.

We saw this in full effect in the United States at "Trump Rallies" in 2016-2020, and we see it anywhere a population of people with imperial worldviews feel unfairly treated and are looking for a "strongman" leader who promises to "defeat their enemies."

Most people reading this book do not have a primary Imperial worldview and therefore may find this Autocratic style of leadership unappealing, or even feel a strong aversion to it. But you must remember, everyone doesn't think like you do. Always remember that people with an Imperial worldview love autocratic leaders. In fact, they see Autocratic leadership as the only legitimate form of leadership.

Let's take a closer look at this and use our newfound "worldview lenses" to see how the other three mindsets view this Autocratic leadership style.

People who primarily identify with the Affiliative mindset (the Postmodern worldview) find the Autocratic style appalling and think such leaders should not be allowed to lead; they should be stripped of power.

People who primarily identify with the Traditional mindset believe these "power-centric" folks have lost their way and need to be "saved." In their mind, what these "lost souls" need is Jesus (or Allah depending on the culture their parents raised them in). This "save the lost souls" mentality is the basis of popular traditional programs such as the "12-Step" recovery programs which are quite useful for power-centric and traditional addicts but really risky for people with modern and postmodern worldviews.

Some Traditionals do vote for autocrats if they believe the autocrats holds their same ethnocentric beliefs, and if they believe the autocrat's claims that he will defeat their enemies. We see this with right-wing "Nationalists" movements wherever they are found. (Many examples of this have been seen in recent years, not only in the United States but also in Europe, Australia and across Asia).

However, the moment that Traditionalists recognize that the self-serving, manipulative autocrat does not actually share their traditional beliefs, they then see the same leader as immoral, and one who should be stripped of power. To invoke our familiar example from recent American history, this was seen when a subset of right-wing Republicans and gullible evangelicals realized that they had been hoodwinked, and instantly transformed from red cap-wearing MAGA loyalists to "Never Trumpers."

What about Achievers? How do they view the Autocratic leadership style?

People who primarily identify with the Achiever mindset consider the Autocratic style to be a bit extreme, but a potentially useful tool for difficult employees or suppliers that won't respond to any other tactics.

Understandably, many new students of integrally-informed approaches to leadership have difficulty imagining themselves using the Autocratic leadership style.

However, the truth is that people who primarily identify with the Power mindset are extremely unlikely to respond to the Strategic, Humanistic or Authoritarian leadership styles.

What do you do if you encounter, or manage, these Power-centric folks?

Integrally-informed leaders understand the importance of recognizing this mindset when they encounter it, and if necessary, drawing upon aspects of the Autocratic style (hopefully in judicial combination with other styles) to connect with, influence and motivate people who only respect this style. In this section, I introduced you to the key concepts of matching leadership styles to follower mindsets. Next, I want to discuss benchmarking.

Benchmarking Leadership Ability

Peter Drucker famously said, "If you can't measure it, you can't manage it." Many of the articles with titles that sound something like "why most leadership development programs fail" include this issue of measurement. Most leadership training companies use a kind of "smoke and mirrors" tactic to suggest that they measure when they actually don't. Do you know what it is?

Rather than measure the actual performance of the leaders (before and after) the training, and compare results or actual outcomes, they run bogus "participant surveys" and simply ask the participants how they "feel" about the training, are the "satisfied" with the training, and do they think they training might "benefit" their leadership. You don't have to be a PhD statistician to see how utterly bogus this approach is. What they do not do is measure actual leadership behaviors (much less leadership outcomes) before and after these programs.

You may wonder if these leadership training companies are being intentionally deceptive?

I do not think so. I've studied this problem and have become convinced that the reason they do not attempt to measure specific leadership behaviors is they <u>do not teach</u> specific leadership behaviors. Further, most leadership trainers and coaches can't even tell you what effective leadership behaviors look like, in fact, many can't even tell you what leaders actually do.

This comes back to the most fundamental problem with leadership development as it is approached today: most leadership development programs do not even recognize that leadership is a technical and complex skill, therefore they do not even attempt to break the skill down into its component parts. In an earlier example, I used basketball (dribbling, passing, shooting rebounding), baseball (batting, throwing, fielding, running the base), playing a musical instrument (notes, scales, chords, chord progressions) and mixed martial arts (wrestling, striking, grappling). Because most leadership coaching and training programs do not recognize the specific abilities, the skill sets, the techniques (behaviors), they do not teach them, and certainly have no way to measure them.

This massive failure of the leadership development industry is one of the things we must "reinvent" if we are to reform this broken $15B (per year) industry (in the U.S. and closer to $50B worldwide).

You are no doubt familiar with the "gap analysis." If we want to improve an ability, we need to have some kind of reliable measurement or benchmark to compare against and to use to develop training methods, content and evaluate progress over time.

To my knowledge, reliable proficiency benchmarks for the main areas of leadership responsibility as well as the essential leadership skills (for each), are not available anywhere beyond this book.

There are some rudimentary assessments available that I don't find adequate. There are also some very sophisticated 360 tools for evaluating leadership psychology that require significant training and an expensive certification to decipher which can be valuable but are not something that individual leaders (such as the readers of this book) can self-administer. To address an important yet unmet need,

I developed the benchmarks for the three "essential leader abilities" and the nine "leadership core competencies" drawn from more than 20,000 hours of experience researching, developing, evaluating, and training thousands of leaders over the last two decades. To keep this book short, I will refer you to my other book entitled: *Integral Leadership: The World's First Unifying Theory of Leadership That Will Forever Transform How You Understand, Practice and Develop Leadership*

Practice Based Leadership

I am revealing to you the exact mechanism that my partners, employees and students have been using for 22 years to get 3X to 5X better results (in terms of leadership skill improvement) over conventional leadership education practices.

It is this:

> *We teach leadership as a practice made up of concrete, specific discreet techniques. We de-emphasize concepts and we focus on the specific techniques, the practices that lead to skills, that are common to all outstanding leaders. While we do draw on best practices, we contextualize them to make sure we are using the right approach (and leadership style) with the right people and circumstances.*

It begins with treating leadership like yoga, painting, martial arts, dance or any other complex skill that practitioners deliberately practice in a very specific way.

"Deliberate practice" is the method that surgeons, professional athletes, and peak performers use to quickly learn and internalize new skills. We have used it for 20 years, helping leaders rapidly adopt new skills with consistent results.

I can summarize deliberate practice with three main ideas.

1) *You must train "technique"*

To learn a complex skill efficiently, you must isolate the skill and the techniques that make up the skill, set specific goals based on best practices and benchmarks, practice with full attention and push beyond your comfort zone.

2) *You must receive expert mentorship to do the techniques correctly*

This looks like frequent coaching and guidance from people who have mastered the technique and know how to teach it. Facilitators and coaches must be experts in the specific techniques.

3) *You must obtain feedback to calibrate and improve*

This aspect of deliberate practice involves obtaining immediate feedback (from qualified experts) to be able to calibrate and fine tune the technique as you internalize and habitualize it. The first technique has to be correct before layering on the next. And the next has to be correct before layering on the one that follows it.

This is the essence of "Practice-Based Leadership" which is the method that my partners and I pioneered 22 years ago.

I am not going to mince words here. Do not spend another dollar with so-called leadership development experts who aren't experts in the specific techniques of leadership that you need to learn to improve your skills.

You would <u>never</u> hire a guitar teacher or a baseball coach who can't play guitar or who isn't a terrific baseball player (or who doesn't know which techniques to teach you, or who talks about the "qualities" or "traits" of great guitar or baseball players). Don't hire leadership trainers or coaches who do that either!

To break it down further into the techniques, you wouldn't go into a baseball "batting cage" to train on that skill with someone who is a "mindset coach" or "life coach" or "executive coach" who has never swung a bat (much less possesses the expert level proficiency of doing the technique perfectly).

Imagine a martial arts or baseball coach who only talked to you about mindset and asked you a lot of reflection questions but didn't teach you how to correctly practice your new techniques, or worse, didn't even know the techniques in the first place?

Kind of obvious when you think about it, right?

Repetition is the mother of skill. So, I will repeat this crucial point.

> *The only effective way to learn technical and complex skills (baseball, basketball, playing a musical instrument, martial arts, flying an airplane or leadership) is to break the ability down into its component parts or "skill sets" and then train, memorize and internalize each of those techniques until they become second nature.*

Learning complex skills follows a pattern that looks like this. Again, you already know this because you have already mastered numerous complex skills. So let me remind you what you already know.

Over many weeks, practices become habits. Over many months, habits become skills. With time and ongoing practice, those skills combine into "skill sets." Ultimately, the skill sets come together to form the "ability" (the complex skill) that the learner is practicing.

To be competent at baseball, an athlete must have the skills to throw, catch, hit and run. To be competent at MMA, an athlete must have wrestling, kickboxing, and grappling skills.

For the past 22+ years, all of my leadership trainings have used "Deliberate Practice" principles from "Expert Performance Theory." This is central to why my leadership trainings consistently produce results where most leadership training programs fail.

Two decades ago, I was the first to apply *Expert Performance Theory* and *Deliberate Practice* to leadership development at Integral Institute (where I was a senior faculty member) and the Stagen Leadership Academy (that I co-founded) when I created the original "Integral Leadership Program." That program is still running 22 years later (and still going strong).

As pioneers in this practice-based approach to leadership development, is safe to say that my partners and I have more experience than anyone else in the world with it.

We literally invented the category of "practice based leadership."

I have personally spent 20 hours a week, 50 weeks a year for over 20 years training, mentoring, and coaching leaders, totaling around 1,000 hours per year. The "10,000 hour rule," popularized by Malcolm Gladwell's book "Outliers," suggests that it takes about 10,000 hours for someone to become an expert or master a complex skill such as medicine, martial arts, management, or leadership. I have logged more than 10,000 hours *training leaders* and additional 10,000 hours *coaching leaders*, for a total of over 20,000 hours. This provides me with a breadth of relevant experience and depth of understanding of leadership development that very few people have.

I am not telling you this to impress you. I am telling you this to impress upon you that the information in this book is coming from someone who has vast experience using these methods and who is a legitimate "expert" as defined by Expert Performance Theory. I am telling you this in the hopes of motivating and inspiring you to adopt these methods and use them in your own leadership development and in your organization.

These methods work, and they work better than most of the other leadership development methods you are likely to encounter.

All of this experience has led me to one crucial conclusion: *the only effective way to learn the complex skill we call leadership is to use a technique- and practice-based approach.*

This insight and this belief flies in the face of convention.

Approximately 80-90% of the leadership training programs on the market focus on character traits, abstract "qualities" of leaders, and vague concepts like "EQ" yet offer no specific techniques or skills to practice to develop emotional intelligence. (More on EQ later.)

The straight truth is this: To learn complex skills, especially leadership, you need training on individual techniques and then you must practice those techniques until they become internalized, and then over time, combine those growing skills together to form new abilities.

The phrase "10,000 hours" is likely familiar to many readers, but few know its origins. It was popularized by Malcom Gladwell in his book *Outliers: The Story of Success,* but the term was originally coined by Anders Ericsson, who researched and developed the method called "Deliberate Practice." Ericsson's research showed that only certain types of practice lead to high-performance or expert-level skills, not all practice.

When you leverage this method called "deliberate practice" in our management and leadership skill learning efforts, you can expect to dramatically increase the rate at which you can level up abilities. And while it could take 5-10 years to achieve that 10,000 hour "expert" level performance in leadership skills, we can expect massive gains in performance in just half a year to a year if you follow the guidelines that "expert performance theory" and this book explain.

My experience shows that following my Accelerating Leadership method (which in my programs includes micro learning tutorial videos and weekly group coaching on Zoom), a leader can go from beginner to intermediate, or intermediate to expert in only about 6-12 months. If you apply all the things you are learning in this book series (all four books), even without the benefit of my micro-learning tutorial videos and my group coaching on Zoom, you could still go from beginner to intermediate or intermediate to expert level in just a couple of years.

There is an old saying that goes, "Practice makes perfect".

Like so many old sayings, this one points to something true and useful, but isn't really accurate. Sure, practice is important and certainly helpful. But if you are practicing in any way other than the perfect "form" then that is actually reinforcing wrong technique.

Learning the wrong form of a technique is hardly what any reasonable person would call "makes perfect".

So, we can correct that misconception by restating it this way... *Perfect practice makes perfect.*

This idea of "perfect practice" is not just a figure of speech. Nor does it point merely to the correct form of a technique mentioned previously. "Perfect practice" is about a very specific type of practice that dramatically accelerates learning and crushes the steep learning curves associated with complex skills.

While this relatively new kind of "practice" is starting to gain popularity, most people have either never heard of it, or have perhaps heard of it but don't know how to engage it and use it.

As mentioned prior, the person who pioneered much of the research in this area and coined the term "Deliberate Practice" was Anders Ericsson. He has written several books, but I will highlight two here.

They are: *The Cambridge Handbook of Expertise and Expert Performance* and *Peak: Secrets from the New Science of Expertise.*

Ericsson's research suggests that only certain types of practice can lead to expertise. George Leonard also described a similar concept in his book: *Mastery: The Keys to Success and Long-Term Fulfillment.* I will use Anders Ericsson's own words to define and clarify exactly what deliberate practice is...

> *"Deliberate practice develops skills that other people have already figured out how to do and for which effective training techniques have been established. The practice regimen should be designed and overseen by a teacher or coach who is familiar with the abilities of expert performers and with how those abilities can best be developed."*

Ericsson found that surgeons, for example, use deliberate practice, which involves specific goals and immediate feedback. Surgeons can see how their actions impact their patient's health and make improvements quickly.

Radiologists, on the other hand, don't have the same connection between their diagnosis and the outcome (the long-term health of their patients). While this example highlights the critical importance of specific goals and feedback, Ericsson strongly emphasizes that it's not enough to merely mirror the behaviors of the experts.

It's important to understand the thinking, the reasoning and the feelings behind those behaviors. In plain terms, it's not enough to just parrot behaviors that would be how the behavior looks from the outside. You must also understand how that technique feels from the inside. What does the expert, the exemplar, think and feel when they are performing the technique?

Ericsson's research showed that the quality of these internal representations separates experts from novices. This applies to every field they have studied, including rock climbing, music, sports, research, writing, memory skills, and sales.

It's important to note that you cannot create optimal "internal representations" (how the technique is experienced from the inside) just by doing an activity over and over again. Rather, you need to model the internal representations of an exemplar who has the skill you want to acquire. This is why I will frequently remind you throughout this book that the fastest way to learn leadership skills is to get mentoring, guidance and coaching from people who are experts in those specific techniques.

To truly understand a skill, it's not enough to just hear about it or read about it, you must experience it and practice it over and over until it becomes habit. This is one of the main reasons that most leadership development programs fail to develop leader. They usually teach the wrong things in the wrong way. If they aren't teaching specific skills then they aren't actually helping people get better at the technical and complex skill called leadership.

To progress in your leadership skills, your facilitators and coaches must be experts in both the techniques they are teaching and the best methods to teach those techniques. If their "leadership model" does not emphasize specific techniques and practices, and if their advice to help leaders get better at the technical and complex skill of leadership does not incorporate "deliberate practice," then I strongly suggest you look elsewhere.

Further, if your leadership trainer or coach is not a "black belt" (an expert) in the techniques they are coaching you in, then they are not qualified to coach you.

You must get this.

> *If you spend money on leadership coaches who are not experts in the specific skills of leadership, then you are wasting your time and your money. And this includes the ubiquitous "mindset coaches" who will happily take your money but can't teach you anything about leadership. People who say "mindset is everything" don't know much about anything. Mindset is most definitely not everything. Its not even the main thing. Mindset is 20% at most. Strategy and technique is 80% or more of what leads to success in any endeavor.*

Mindset coaching is mainly helpful for people <u>who already know how to do a technique perfectly</u> and they are trying to adopt the best psychology (mindset) to help them do it more consistently. Mindset coaching is great for professional athletes who are already at the very top of their game and who know the techniques well.

Executive coaches and self-described leadership coaches who focus primarily on mindset, in my experience, do this because the do not know the strategies, skills or techniques of leadership.

In my opinion, if they did know the techniques of leadership, they would be sharing them with their clients (a lot more than mindset). To be blunt, focusing on mindset is a primary way that unqualified leadership coaches cover up their lack of knowledge about leadership. Do them a favor and share this book with them. Maybe they will choose to level up their knowledge about leadership.

As mentioned earlier in this book, leadership advice-givers can't agree on a single definition of effective leadership because they have different worldviews and as such, see different approaches (or styles) of leadership as more appealing (based on the values, assumptions and beliefs inherent in their specific worldview). I spent over a decade working with Ken Wilber at Integral Institute and my R&D team at Stagen Leadership Academy, and more than a million of dollars developing and testing the "Unifying Theory of Leadership" that provides the theoretical foundation for this work.

This short book summarizes the resulting breakthroughs in understanding leadership, instructional design for leadership training programs, and strategies for rapidly raising effective leadership skills. This book discloses this well-kept trade secret, which we've used for nearly two decades to train over 10,000 corporate executives (and many leaders in developing countries through my nonprofit organization).

I hope you can appreciate the value of the research, frameworks, models and tools that you now hold in your hands. I have spent well over a million dollars of my own money, and many millions of dollars of my company's money over a twenty-year period in order to now be in a position to bring you the "simplicity on the other side of complexity" reflected in this model.

I spent five years working with Ken Wilber and Integral Institute to create the original *Unifying Theory of Leadership.* I spent ten additional years testing the model with corporate leaders, simplifying and refining it, resulting in my *Leadership Rosetta Stone.* Then I spent another five years expanding the testing beyond the corporate world to also include international humanitarian efforts, governments, military leaders, religious and even tribal and indigenous leaders in third-world countries, culminating in the *Universal Leadership Model* presented in this book (and my other books).

I tell you this not to impress you; rather, to impress upon you the real value contained in this book that you now own, and hopefully to inspire you to learn, internalize, and most importantly, put into practice these extremely valuable academically-sound, time-tested methods.

In this book, I provide a sufficient overview of the practice-based approach for you to apply in your leadership development efforts (in the "*Teamwork & Culture*" dimension of leadership).

If you want to learn more about this methodology, please see the my book, *Accelerating Leadership: The Groundbreaking Method for Rapid Leadership Development That Achieves Twice the Results in Half the Time at a Fraction of the Cost.*

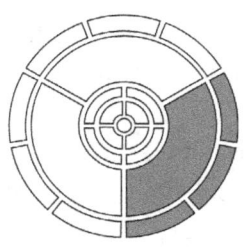

CHAPTER 5: BENCHMARKING TEAMWORK & CULTURE LEADERSHIP CAPACITY

In the "Practice-based Leadership Development Framework" presented previously, I briefly introduced you to this area of responsibility that all leaders share. In this next part of the book, we will take a deeper dive into this dimension, and unpack these three essential skill sets leaders use to fulfill these responsibilities. First, in this short chapter, I will provide you benchmarks for this "overall dimension" of leadership that I call "Teamwork and Culture." So these benchmarks are "high level" for the whole "essential ability" as I also call this dimension. Recall that there are three dimensions of leadership. These were all three summarized previously and I have published one book per dimension. Before we move on to subsequent chapters, where we drill down into each "skill set" in this dimension, it is important to establish benchmarks for this overall "capacity" for "Teamwork and Culture" (as I call it). Also, you will find that in subsequent chapters (one per skill set), I will also provide benchmarks for each of the discrete "skill sets" that leaders utilize in this dimension. Those benchmarks will be more granular (per skill set) as contrasted with this high-level view of a leader's proficiency in the overall "essential ability" we refer to as *Teamwork & Culture."*

A comment about how you "measure up" against these established benchmarks. Given a typical "bell curve," most people fall into the middle range (statistically speaking). Therefore, most readers of this book will likely fall somewhere in the "intermediate" range of proficiency in this essential ability, the dimension I call "Teamwork & Culture." If you were to fall in the lower range, then you have some immediate work to do to avoid undermining your leadership credibility.

My hope is that after reading this book, adopting the best practices outlined here, and engaging these activities in your leadership role with your team for several months, you will begin to see your proficiency inch up from "intermediate" to "late intermediate" and then after a few more months, my hope is that you move into "early advanced" levels of proficiency.

Over time, if you socialize these practices with your team, it is possible to get your whole team into the "advanced" (or "higher levels") of proficiency in this essential ability I am calling Teamwork & Culture.

Once you move into the next chapters on the more granular specific skill sets, you are more likely to find one of them where you (or members of your team or certain teams) fall into the lower range. But let's not get ahead of ourselves. Let's take a moment and get grounded in this essential leadership ability called Culture and Teamwork. (Recall that earlier I also called these three dimensions the "Inherent Leadership Responsibilities." So, let's take an honest look at how your leadership measures up in this essential leadership ability and this inherent responsibility.

Definition

First let's define. The essential leadership ability that I am calling Teamwork & Culture includes all of the activities related to setting your people up for success, creating and maintaining a conducive environment, including a healthy culture and emotional climate, and keeping people engaged and motivated using appropriate and effective communication, including feedback, listening, collaboration and managing conflict.

Making Sure People Work Well Together to Achieve Shared Goals

A well-planned strategy is useless if people don't work together effectively to execute it. Teaming is the ability to build trust, foster collaboration, and create a strong team culture where people feel safe, valued, and motivated. Without strong teaming, even the most talented employees will struggle to perform at their best.

A senior manager skilled in teaming creates an environment where people work together, communicate openly, and stay engaged in their work. They recognize that great teamwork doesn't happen automatically—it must be intentionally built by fostering trust, ensuring clear communication, and keeping employees motivated.

Trust is at the core of strong teamwork. Without trust, employees hesitate to share ideas, avoid asking for help, and struggle to collaborate. A great leader actively builds trust by being transparent, setting clear expectations, and treating employees fairly. They ensure that team members feel comfortable speaking up, raising concerns, and taking initiative without fear of blame or punishment.

Communication is another key part of teaming. A leader who excels in teaming ensures that information flows freely and clearly between teams. They create systems for regular updates, encourage open discussions, and address conflicts before they escalate.

Miscommunication is one of the biggest barriers to effective teamwork, and strong leaders ensure that everyone is on the same page, aligned on priorities, and able to work through disagreements professionally.

Motivation is the final piece of great teamwork. A leader skilled in teaming understands what drives their employees and helps them connect their work to a larger purpose. They celebrate wins, provide opportunities for growth, and ensure that employees feel valued and challenged. Without motivation, teams lose energy and engagement, leading to lower performance and high turnover.

For example, consider a senior manager overseeing a customer service department. Without strong teaming, different teams may work in isolation, employees may feel undervalued, and customer satisfaction may suffer. But by building trust, improving communication, and fostering motivation, the manager creates a high-performance team that collaborates seamlessly and delivers outstanding results.

Teaming is the foundation of organizational success. Leaders who master this ability create workplaces where employees thrive, collaborate effectively, and stay engaged—leading to better outcomes for both teams and the company as a whole.

It is helpful to orient our thinking about this crucial dimension of leadership by reviewing some of the key questions, challenges, and goals that leaders have when addressing this area of leadership.

Building a High-Functioning Team Environment

Teaming is not just about making people work together—it's about intentionally designing the structure, tone, and conditions that allow teams to succeed. In your leadership framework, the Teaming dimension reflects a senior leader's ability to create the right team environment based on their leadership style, team composition, and organizational context. It's not about being emotionally expressive or building "psychological safety"—that only applies to certain follower paradigms. Instead, it's about establishing clarity, rhythm, motivation, and structure that fits the people and the work. This dimension becomes especially important for leaders who manage managers. Frontline teamwork may happen on its own, but high-level coordination across functions, personalities, and teams requires intentionality. Without a well-constructed team environment, even smart and capable people struggle. Misunderstandings fester. Motivation fades. Performance drops. People default to working in silos—not because they don't care, but because no one has built the environment required for them to function as a unit.

The Teaming dimension is composed of three distinct leadership skill sets:

1. Creating the Container (building the team structure and culture and a conducive operating environment)
2. Communication (ensuring clarity, framing, and shared understanding)
3. Motivation (keeping energy, engagement, and effort consistent over time)

When these skills are weak or missing, teams operate with confusion and inconsistency. Leaders manage reactively, performance is uneven, and team culture becomes something accidental or unstable. In contrast, when this dimension is strong, the following outcomes become visible and measurable:

1. Team Clarity – Clear roles, expectations, and structure that support execution.
2. Information Flow – Messages are well-framed, aligned, and understood.

3. Sustained Energy – Teams remain motivated, focused, and engaged under pressure.

Leaders who excel in this dimension don't create one-size-fits-all environments. They create systems and rhythms that fit their team's worldview and leadership style. They reduce confusion, reinforce expectations, and maintain performance over time. The result is not just harmony—it's team resilience, clarity, and momentum.

It is helpful to orient our thinking about this crucial dimension of leadership by reviewing some of the key questions, challenges, and goals that leaders have when addressing this area of leadership.

Teamwork & *Culture Questions*

The following are common questions leaders ask in this dimension.

- What are the best ways to set people up for success with the right kind of team structure and culture?

- How can we improve our feedback and performance reviews?

- How can we deal with people's assumptions and interpretations and avoid misunderstandings?

- What are the best ways to keep people engaged and motivated especially with a diverse workforce?

Teamwork & Culture Challenges

The following are common challenges leaders report in this dimension.

- Low team or department morale (frustrated, discouraged, resentful)

- Low employee engagement or disengagement (low trust or toxic culture)

- Diversity / equity / inclusion issues

- How to manage remote workers and blended workforce (managing on Zoom)

- People are afraid to make mistakes or afraid to take initiative or take risks

- Reassuring the workforce in difficult times that are intimidating, stressful or demoralizing

- Want to change culture but don't know how to shift to the desired culture

- Managers / leaders don't know how to motivate people

- Culture that emphasizes extrinsic motivators fails to tap into intrinsic motivation

- Difficulty motivating a diverse workforce, team members seem unmotivated, How can they be reached? Guarded, defensive or ineffective communication (gaps in listening, dialog, collaboration skills)

- Not enough feedback, ineffective or unbalanced feedback

- Interpersonal or personality conflicts or team rivalries

- Change management, aligning process, messaging and cultural interventions with change

Teamwork & Culture Goals

The following are common goals leaders report in this dimension.

- Do a better job of setting up new team members for success (training, tools, structure)

- Get better at setting the right emotional tone for a positive and conducive working environment

- Getting better at motivating people and keeping morale high on teams

- We must get better at feedback (right way, right amount, in balance to keep people learning and motivated)

- More trust on our team(s) so we can have more honest and open dialog and more fruitful collaboration

- Get better at listening and dialog so we can improve our collaboration skills

- Do better working with assumptions and interpretations to avoid misunderstandings and conflict

Precision Proficiency Benchmarking

A leader's skill proficiency in any of these dimensions is determined less by looking at the leader, a better gauge of the leader's proficiency is to look at the results observed in the organization. Therefore, on the following pages you will find the benchmarks to use when evaluating a leader and their team or organization's current capability in this dimension. These organizational benchmarks are very helpful to use when asking members of a team to self-assess the team's current capabilities. Not only does this provide valuable insights to the leaders, but it also is a terrific conversation starter that you can use to discuss this aspect of the team's (or department or organization's) strengths and gaps which could be elevated to support the group's ability to achieve its shared objectives.

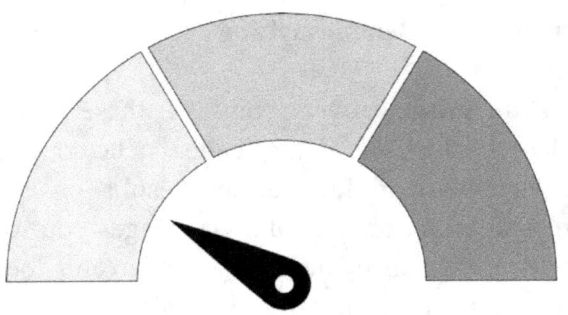

TEAMWORK & CULTURE LOWER RANGE

Leaders at this proficiency level do not actively shape a conducive team environment. There may be occasional wins, but performance is inconsistent and unpredictable. Roles and "lanes" are ambiguous, team members operate in silos, and the culture lacks cohesion. Communication breakdowns and conflict are common, and motivation relies on individual self-drive rather than intentional leadership effort.

- Roles, lanes, and norms are unclear or not reinforced
- Communication is inconsistent across leaders and team
- Motivation is not actively managed; energy fluctuates without intervention
- Culture is emergent, unstructured, or misaligned with performance needs

Leader Self-Description:

We need to do a better job of setting people up for success. While we do have a few strong performers, many of our team members are not engaged or are unmotivated. Communication skills are not our strong suit. It is unclear to me how to motivate this team to embrace high-performance teamwork.

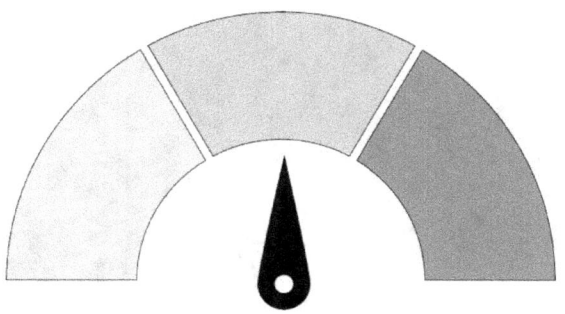

TEAMWORK & CULTURE INTERMEDIATE RANGE

At this intermediate level of proficiency in this ability, leaders begin are more deliberate about creating a conducive team environment. Roles and lanes are more explicit, and communication efforts are more consistent, though still uneven across teams. Some motivational strategies are used, but not consistently or systematically. The team functions moderately well, but the leader's influence on the environment is still limited.

- Some expectations and cultural norms are defined, but not reinforced consistently
- Communication framing improves, but clarity still varies across messages or audiences
- Motivation techniques are applied, but impact is unpredictable
- Teams function acceptably, but momentum stalls or dips frequently

Leader Self-Description:

We enjoy a healthy culture with decent trust and teamwork. We would like to be better at motivating our team members and keeping people highly engaged. In terms of communication, some team members are good listeners, give effective feedback and know how to dialogue, but for others, communication often seems awkward or strained.

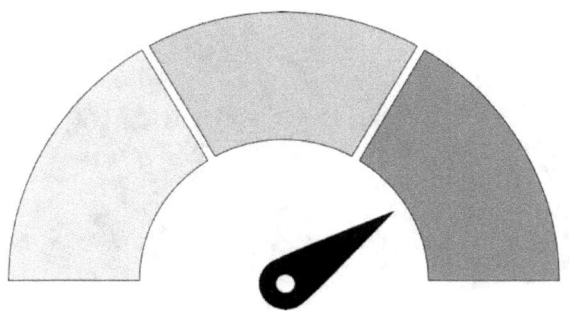

TEAMWORK & CULTURE HIGHER RANGE

Leaders at this level are intentional, consistent, and disciplined in how they construct and manage the team environment. They build and reinforce norms, structure, and communication rhythms that drive performance. They tailor motivational strategies to their team and context, and they continuously shape the environment to support results.

- Leaders deliberately create a conducive team environment with clear structures and an empowering culture (based on needs)
- Communication is well-framed and supports alignment across functions
- Motivation systems are calibrated to the team's worldview
- The team environment supports sustained energy, cohesion, and execution

Leader Self-Description:

Communication, teamwork and culture, in general, are our greatest strengths. Most of our people report that they feel well-equipped, well-trained, empowered and supported. Overall, our team members are highly motivated and engaged and we consistently practice effective communication in the areas of feedback, listening, dialog, collaboration, conflict management and so on.

Now that you have grounded in the levels of proficiency (low, intermediate and high) in this overall dimension, we will move into the subsequent chapters, one per skill set, and we will review the benchmarks for those specific skill sets and many of the most important and most helpful skills, techniques, tools and practices that bolster a leader's ability in each of these skill sets. The first skill set is "Creating the Container."

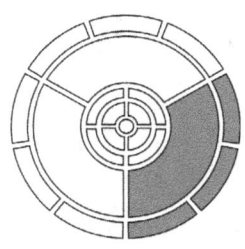

CHAPTER 6: CREATING THE CONTAINER

First we begin with a clear definition and the benchmarks for levels of proficiency in this skill set. I define this skill set by say, "Creating the Container is concerned with your ability to set people up for success—this includes equipping teams with the structure, culture, training, tools and support they need to achieve shared organizational goals."

Team Discussion

When you initiate a conversation with your employees and team(s), you could use some version of the following questions.

- How do we (as managers and as an organization) set people up for success?

- How do we structure teams and cultivate effective teamwork?

- How do we approach culture?

- How do we approach training support for our teammates (and teams)?

Benchmarks

Next we move into the benchmarks for this skill set.

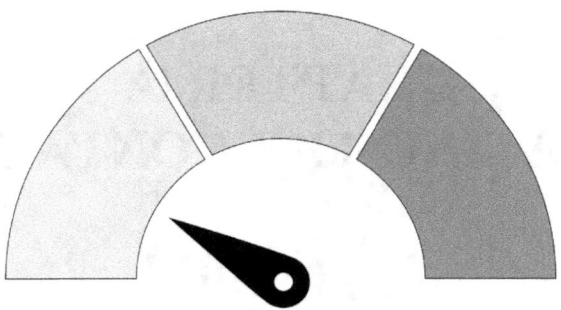

CREATING THE CONTAINER LOWER RANGE

A leader and a team functioning in the lower range of proficiency in this skill set might describe it this way.

Our team, including the culture, happened organically over time. While we try to provide our members with the basic tools they need to do their job, we haven't done a great job of setting people up for success. There isn't a clear structure or identity as a team, and people mainly focus on just doing their jobs as individual contributors.

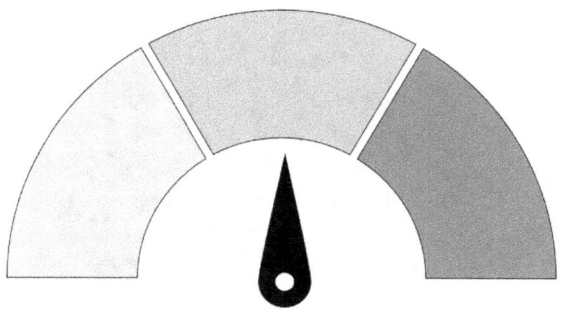

CREATING THE CONTAINER MIDDLE RANGE

A leader and a team functioning in the lower range of proficiency in this skill set might describe it this way.

We have put energy and some investment into enhancing our teamwork. While we did not necessarily design our culture in a deliberate way, we have a pretty good culture. However, it is clear that there is room for improvement on how we can cultivate effective teamwork and an empowered organizational culture.

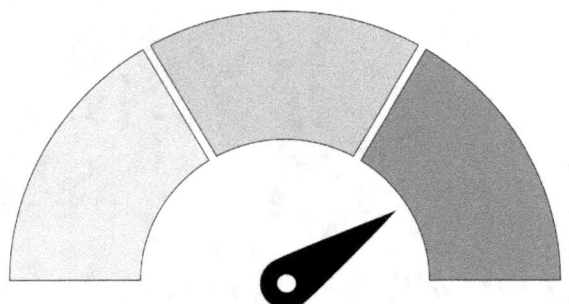

CREATING THE CONTAINER HIGHER RANGE

A leader and a team functioning in the higher range of proficiency in this skill set might describe it this way.

We have invested heavily into teamwork and culture and consider it to be one of our greatest strengths. The majority of our team members would report that they feel well-equipped, well-trained and supported. Our team members are proud to be part of the team and take pride in their high-performance teamwork.

Organizational Structure Primer

We use the term "Creating the Container" to refer to the activities concerned with setting people up for success.

This includes equipping team members with the tools and training they need to do their job well, and it also includes providing the support, structure, and culture that will empower them to work effectively as a team and achieve individual and collective success.

Different leadership experts may use different words to describe these activities, including setting up the structure, organizing a function, establishing a team, putting the conditions in place for desired culture, or giving employees the tools they need to do their job, but they are all pointing to a similar set of activities that fall under the umbrella topic we call Creating the Container.

If you have ever found yourself in a role and didn't feel that you had been "set up for success" by your boss, then you certainly know firsthand how problematic this can be. In that case, you found yourself in a role in a "container" that someone else set up.

Now, in your role as a manager or leader, the responsibility for "creating the container" falls on your shoulders. You may think, "the organizational structure is already set," or, "I feel like I inherited this container."

This is a completely understandable line of thinking. It is true that when you stepped into your current role, there was a structure, a container, and a team in place. In that sense, you did inherit the "container" the day you stepped into your current role.

It is also true that since that first day, you are now a manager or leader in that container. It is now your container. You share the responsibility with the other managers or leaders in your group to be "creating the container" ongoing.

Organizational structures, teams, interpersonal dynamics and culture are not static. Organizations are made up of humans, relationships, behavior patterns, assumptions and expectations, and an internal and external environment that is continually changing.

This is why we do not refer to this collection of activities and competencies as "Create the Container" as if you do it once and forget it. Leaders are responsible for the conditions in which their people work. These conditions are not static, they are dynamic.

Therefore, you are always "Creating the Container" with every decision you make, with every meeting you run, with every piece of feedback you offer your co-workers, with every assignment you delegate, with every coaching or training session you conduct, and the list goes on.

You are always "creating the container" whether you are doing it deliberately and consciously, or whether you are doing it without realizing it, unconsciously.

While it is human nature to look for excuses or blame the broader organization or some other leader for the current structure, culture, team and organizational dynamics at play, if you are the leader of your team or manager of your area, then it is in fact your job to set your people up for success.

Leaders set the pace, set the tone, and yes, create the culture. So it is unlikely that anyone else is in a position to gain more clarity on the challenges or gaps that may exist in your current "container," and where the opportunities and leverage might be.

Organizational Design

Organization Design is a process for shaping the way organizations are structured and operated.

It involves many different aspects of organization dynamics, including forming, structuring and restructuring teams, reporting structures, decision-making procedures, communication channels, and more.

From time to time, a large-scale reorganization is necessary. At other points, more subtle shifts in structures and systems can ensure that an organization continues to have the necessary "conditions for success" in place.

There are many potential benefits when an organization, a department, or a team's structures and systems are well-designed. Some of these benefits include:

- Increased efficiency

- Faster and more effective decision making

- Improved quality of products and services

- Safer working conditions

- A happier, healthier and more motivated workforce

- Greater preparedness for current and future challenges

However, if the current organizational design is either outdated or insufficient in some way, an organization can suffer serious issues, including:

- Lack of coordination between different parts of the organization

- Ineffective problem solving or decision-making

- Inconsistent quality of work

- Low morale, leading to high staff turnover

- Disappointing performance

- Missed targets

- Career setbacks for individuals or the leaders of the organization

Even if a particular container was effective in the past, that doesn't mean it will remain so forever or even for long. Leaders need to continually monitor and adjust the organizational structure to ensure that the "conditions for success" are still adequately in place.

Fundamental Types of Organizational Designs

When the Design of the Organization is Due for Change

There are three common scenarios that trigger the need for a change in the organizational design.

1. A Significant Internal or External Change

A key person may exit the organization, or the department or group needs a different structure to meet an internal need such as adopting a new function or activity. Another internal example is when new equipment or technology has been adopted that changes how work is conducted.

Examples of external changes would include a new competitor or rival putting pressure on the organization to function differently or a change in regulations that require new organizational activities to comply.

2. New Organizational Strategy or Goals

The leaders of the broader organization might steer the organization in a new direction, or may set priorities that require your team or department to adapt. Perhaps your organization has new goals or a new way of defining or measuring success.

3. The Current Organizational Design is Outdated or Insufficient

Many aspects of change affecting an organization are gradual, but from time to time an inflection point is reached. For example, perhaps over time you have increased your people's flexible working options, but issues have surfaced, such as deadlines or milestones being missed or quality issues emerging.

You may reach a point where you need another layer of management, or perhaps you need to either split up a work group or merge two groups to more effectively achieve the evolving organizational objectives.

Team Development Primer

One essential element of "creating the container" is to be deliberate about how the team is set up and managed. One of the most central ideas inherent to this discussion is how team dynamics change over time.

In this section, we want to briefly prime an ongoing discussion on what can be referred to as "team development." There are numerous excellent models for framing how team dynamics change over time, but perhaps the best known, and one that is still extremely useful comes from Bruce Tuckman who introduced it all the way back in 1965.

The Stages of Team Development

Effective leaders are deliberate about how the team is set up and managed. One of the most central ideas inherent to this discussion is how team dynamics change over time.

In this section, we want to briefly prime an ongoing discussion on what can be referred to as "team development".

There are numerous excellent models for framing how team dynamics change over time, but perhaps the best known, and one that is still extremely useful comes from Bruce Tuckman who introduced it all the way back in 1965.

Tuckman discovered that while each team is unique in many ways, they all seem to go through four phases that have enough in common that they can be identified, named and discussed.

Each stage has different characteristics, needs, challenges and opportunities. We will briefly summarize each of Tuckman's phases, then we will go more deeply into the characteristics and dynamics of each stage, including what you can do as the team leader to boost teamwork, trust, cooperation and performance at each stage over time.

Forming Stage

In this stage, team members come together and begin to get to know each other. Initial roles, activities and expectations surface. Team goals and approaches (strategies and tactics) are socialized. Members begin to explore the boundaries of acceptable group behavior as individuals begin to see themselves as members of the team.

Team dynamics, leadership and collaboration styles are established, both formally and informally. All of these things are happening whether members or leaders are thinking about them consciously or being deliberate about them.

Storming Stage

Once the forming stage is complete, teams can be expected to move into the storming phase.

Team members have their own ideas as to their preferences about the process and they have their own individual goals, expectations and personal agendas.

Storming is one of the most difficult stages for the team. Members begin to experience the nuance of how the work is done, how tasks are delegated, and how people communicate and coordinate.

In the process, gaps are identified when there is a lack of clarity or confusion about roles, expectations or differences in styles.

People may feel frustrated, impatient, disappointed or discouraged when things don't go smoothly, as planned or how they imagined the team dynamics would be.

It is normal for some conflicts to arise. It is crucial for teams to handle this phase skillfully so that the "wrinkles can be ironed out" without undermining trust, credibility or morale. Effective leadership is crucial at this stage.

Norming Stage

The Norming phase is when the team begins to stabilize. The members have reached a shared understanding of how they work together, how tasks are delegated and completed, and the specific processes become routine (or normal).

Working relationships are solidified, communication starts to feel more natural and becomes more effective (and takes less time than in the previous stage).

Members come to accept the team's ground rules, roles and expectations. Conflict reduces and people start to act less competitively and more cooperatively.

Performing Stage

In the Performing stage, the team has settled into its routines, processes, relationships and expectations.

Now that all those things have become normalized, and there is some consistency over time, the team can step back and identify the things that work the best and the things that can be adjusted to enhance performance.

Team members have discovered and accepted each other's strengths and weaknesses in their specific roles and how the roles interact.

It should be obvious that teams simply can't perform at their best until they have completed the prior three development stages.

The Four Phases of High-Performance Teamwork

We will now build on the excellent foundation that Bruce Tuckman has provided us with his straightforward *"Forming, Storming, Norming and Performing"* stages, and propose a slightly more nuanced model that also has four phases that track closely with Tuckman's while adding quite a bit more detail and guidance for team leaders.

While effective teamwork is certainly the goal of every team leader, in this expanded framework, we will look closely at some of the additional factors that can support what many leaders call "high-performance teamwork".

High-performance teams are never created overnight.

Rather, they progressively and incrementally increase their willingness and skill at cooperating and performing over a period of time.

Most organizational experts and experienced team leaders recognize some version of stages, or phases, of teamwork.

In addition to Tuckman's framework, several other prominent and useful models have been incorporated and integrated into the "Four Phases of High-Performance Teamwork" presented here.

First, we will summarize some of the most crucial activities the team must accomplish at each of the four phases before they can mature into the next phase.

Following is a high-level overview of the milestones for each of these phases.

The Alignment Phase (Developmental Milestones)

Teams must fulfill the following activities in this stage before moving on to the next:

1. Clarify values, purpose, and vision.

2. Set realistic, quantifiable objectives.

3. Clarify roles and responsibilities.

4. Organize for effectiveness.

5. Establish team guidelines.

The Identification Phase (Developmental Milestones)

Teams must fulfill the following activities in this phase before making it to the next:

1. Refine roles and responsibilities.

2. Manage conflict skillfully, further clarify expectations and re-establish accountability.

3. Cultivate and solidify team identity.

The Collaboration Phase (Developmental Milestones)

Teams must complete the following activities before moving on to the next:

1. Learn how this unique team performs best.

2. Develop feedback paths.

3. Leverage increasing autonomy for higher performance

The High-Performance Phase (Developmental Milestones)

Teams must complete the following tasks before moving on to the next:

1. Anticipate each other's behavior and operate with extreme efficiency

2. Encourage innovative thinking

3. Solve problems quickly

4. Practice team "renewal"

Now that we have provided a brief overview of the activities and developmental milestones that teams must accomplish in each phase, we will take a more granular look at the activities that teams must engage in as they progress through these phases over many months, or in some cases, even years.

As mentioned before, not all teams get to the later phases.

You can identify where your team is currently and use the information provided in this section to understand what you can do, and may need to do, in order to complete the phase you are currently in.

In this next section, we will go back through the same four phases and offer some additional tips and guidelines to help you achieve the developmental milestones for each stage.

This information will also give you some idea of the activities that lie ahead if you and your team do progress to the next phase.

How to Complete the Alignment Phase

In the alignment, or forming phase, team member compliance tends to be high.

Yet goals may be unclear and communication may be guarded.

Team subgroups rarely exist, largely because team members tend to avoid conflict and minimize differences at this early stage.

For groups to complete this phase and climb to higher levels of performance, they must clarify purpose and process, and get all members moving in the same direction.

Key practices during the Alignment Phase include:

1. Clarify the purpose and vision

These elements may seem obvious, and it may be tempting not to capture them formally. However, having these directional statements in writing helps avoid misunderstandings and eliminates many potential negative conflicts. By clarifying the team's purpose and vision in a formal way, the members of the team will understand the "what" and "why" that define and determine team success.

2. Set realistic, quantifiable objectives

Teams must have clear and well-defined objectives – an "end game." These objectives must be aligned with the team's purpose and vision. In keeping with the nature of a given team and the reason for its formation, the objectives must also be realistic and quantifiable. The point of setting these objectives is to allow team members to track progress, receive feedback, and hold each other accountable for results.

3. Clarify roles and responsibilities

Roles should reflect the specific talents of each team member as well as the team's overall sense of itself, and should also coincide with the specific mindsets that are represented and interacting. Try to strike the right balance between members who already possess the necessary talent and those who are likely and ready to develop the talent through their participation in the team.

Clarifying responsibilities can include pre-designating a default decision-making process, such as naming a "final authority," or a "binding arbiter," even if the preferred intent is to approach problems and opportunities collaboratively.

4. Organize for effectiveness

Organizing for effectiveness ensures that the team has all the resources it needs to fulfill its purpose. This may include sufficient budgeting, staffing, IT, and other resources.

The team should secure appropriate decision-making authority in addition to the specific expectations, project deadlines, project management and tracking, and schedule coordination that will maximize team effectiveness.

See the section in this book called Responsibility, Authority and Expectations for more detailed guidelines on this topic.

5. Establish team guidelines

During the Alignment Phase, the team must establish clear expectations and outline guidelines – the "rules of the road." These guidelines will apply to team interactions, project management, frequency of meetings, reporting procedures, the decision-making process, basic work methods, reporting of concerns, and dispute resolution.

Failure to outline clear guidelines at this phase may result in unnecessary conflicts and create obstacles to future productivity when collaborative decision-making becomes more crucial.

How to Complete the Identification Phase

More often than not, newly formed teams drop in performance measures as they break through the civility of the initial formation. For this reason, the Identification Phase is sometimes called the storming phase.

Counter-intuitively, a strong team is actually increasing its effectiveness during this often-rocky time, characterized by increased conflict and tension. Subgroups and coalitions now form, which may break along values or mindset lines, or around some commonly perceived interest.

Leaders should expect to see increased member participation, but decreased conformity and higher role dissatisfaction. Because differences of opinion are now out in the open, attempts to convert or coerce others to a specific viewpoint are frequent. While often well-intentioned, this can be a bit misguided.

Key practices during this phase include:

1. Refining roles and responsibilities

Each team member's respective strengths and limitations come into focus during this phase. Leadership may need to modify team members' roles and responsibilities accordingly. These changes should not be viewed as negative; in fact, many of these shifts are the direct result of the team working toward maximum effectiveness.

Leaders of high-performance teams recognize the power of this natural progression and make adjustments that enhance play without throwing off the team's stability.

2. Managing conflict skillfully, further clarifying expectations and re-establishing accountability

Missteps, communication breakdowns, and conflict often accompany this phase. Again, this is natural and should not be viewed negatively, and team members and/or its leader with high emotional intelligence can help this transition go more smoothly.

If the members maintain an environment of mutual trust and respect, most conflicts can be resolved in a way that strengthens bonds and clarifies expectations and accountabilities.

3. Cultivating and solidifying team identity

As the team faces and overcomes challenges together, it will start to solidify. Once the members get past being merely polite to each other and have a chance to face and overcome adversity, they will begin to develop a genuine sense of who they are as a group.

How to Complete the Collaboration Phase

Few teams reach the Collaboration Phase, but those teams that do have moved beyond simple aggregation of individual performances. The team is now ready to step into the genuine risks of conflict, joint effort, and collective action.

During the collaborative phase, the team's goals tend to become clearer as do its sense of priorities. Team members are likely to report a renewed or improved sense of satisfaction.

During this phase, members tend to drop barriers to communication and relax expectations and preconceptions about how things should be done.

They also tend to loosen their need to solve, fix, and control outcomes.

Key practices during this phase include the following.

1. Using observation and reflection to learn how this unique team performs best

As members get to know and understand one another better, the team will find its own unique rhythm, language, and interpersonal groove. As members of an identifiable entity, the team learns how best to collectively engage the leading developmental lines of team members (their strengths), and to compensate for lagging lines (weaknesses).

This increased awareness allows the team to incorporate the contributions of useful mavericks into a more synergistic collective.

The following questions are useful for team members and especially the team leaders to reflect on:

Does the team possess an appropriate mix of talents (problem-solving, technical/functional, and interpersonal)?

Is it small enough in number to be flexible, with an agreement around individual and mutual accountability as part of its priorities?

Does the team have sufficiently specific goals, a common approach, and a meaningful purpose and vision?

2. Developing Feedback Paths

Feedback is essential for effective collaboration.

Clearly, both positive feedback that reinforces desired behavior as well as constructive criticism that offers guidance on how to improve performance when it is below standards or expectations are important.

See the section in this book entitled "Feedback" for specific guidelines and feedback best practices.

3. Leveraging increasing autonomy for higher performance

At this stage, the team is learning how to collaborate effectively in making decisions. They have established an atmosphere of mutual respect, set clear priorities, and are committed to the team's purpose.

A team at this stage knows that each member is effective in his/her role and understands the work well enough to have increasing levels of autonomy (less supervision) and also more decision-making authority to get their work done in the most high-leverage ways.

See the section on "Effective Delegation" for some specific guidelines, including the practice called *"Trust But Verify."*

How to Complete the High-Performance Phase

Even fewer teams reach the High-Performance Phase.

Members of these elite teams may begin to report flow states, and acknowledge a palpable sense of trust, efficiency and effectiveness within the team.

Key practices during this phase include the following.

1. Anticipating each other's behavior and operating with extreme efficiency

Through the growth of team experiences, team members bond and come to know and understand each other on a profound level. This profound level of rapport leads team members to anticipate each other's moves, just as professional athletes do on the playing field.

Within teams, this high level of rapport and communication excellence leads the team to an extremely high level of efficiency.

2. Encouraging innovative thinking

A high level of rapport, trust, and respect, combined with the ability to communicate openly and directly, helps cultivate an environment conducive to innovative thinking.

Teams at this phase will become comfortable discussing diverse perspectives, encouraging and reward creative thinking.

3. Solving problems quickly

The combination of trust, communication, and innovative thinking helps the team become proficient in creative problem-solving. These skills also allow the team to resolve internal conflicts quickly and efficiently.

4. Practicing team renewal

For a high-performance team to remain in top form, it will have to work hard to maintain the skills that led to success.

Just as sports teams have to constantly practice to stay at the top of their game, high-performance teams must engage in frequent renewal activities.

The following "Four Rs" of team renewal serve as a useful guideline.

The Four R's of Team Renewal

Reinvigorate Motivation and Commitment

While a team member may lose focus from time to time, it is the responsibility of the entire team – and especially its leader – to help renew commitment and enthusiasm toward the collective purpose and objectives.

Individual members' personal values and goals are the primary factors motivating them to pursue the team's goals. Consequently, the leader needs to specifically know what motivates each team member. Individual team members must always be able to answer the question, "What's in it for me?"

If a team member gets burned out or discouraged, either the leader, or other team members, should take steps to renew motivation when appropriate. In the case of self-managed teams, members are mindful of each other's motivators and provide support and encouragement as needed.

Revitalize Team Meetings

"Familiarity breeds contempt," as the saying goes.

Over time, team meetings can become routine and boring. Mix it up occasionally and keep things interesting by introducing new and even off-the-wall elements into team meetings. Hold meetings on a boat, at a theme park, or at a weekend retreat.

Routine business meetings can also be enlivened by changing the agenda, having a guest speaker, watching a film clip, listening to thought-provoking music, or throwing in some creativity or team building activities. Use your imagination.

Recognize, Reward, and Celebrate the Team's Success

Celebrating achievements and rewarding successful performance are essential elements in rejuvenating team enthusiasm and commitment. Hosting a semiannual or annual awards banquet, or its equivalent, can provide much needed long-term perspective on a team's achievements and success.

Reconnect with Values, Purpose, and Vision

Eventually, the "honeymoon phase" of any relationship ends.

Over time, people can become jaded – high-performance teams are no different.

In the same way that married couples "renew their vows", teams can periodically reconnect with what is most important to them – their values, purpose, and vision.

This may be a good time to revise the team's directional statements or "stakeholder alignment" statements including values, purpose, and/or vision statements.

Those are the "Four R's" of Team Renewal that will help you keep a team that has reached the high-performance stage in the high-performance stage over time.

In this section, we have learned the four fundamental stages of how teams develop over time, commonly known as "forming, storming, norming and performing."

We also offered a comprehensive reference guide to help you know what you need to do with your team based upon which of these four stages your team is currently in.

Your task as the leader is to accurately identify which stage best describes your current team, and then study the qualities, guidelines and tips to help a team operate effectively at this stage and complete all of the criteria at this phase that will allow the team to proceed to the next level in its development.

This comprehensive section, along with the handout that accompanies this section, represents an important set of guidelines that can serve as a map to guide your team development activities at any stage of development, and refer back often as your team continues to progress.

This section is highly complementary and synergistic with many of the other sections offered in this leadership training. You can use many of the other techniques and skills introduced in this leadership training to help you accomplish the milestones and meet your team's needs at each one of these four stages, depending on the stage that your team is currently working on.

Organizational Drama

The word "drama" has a nearly universal connotation for leaders in organizations.

When you say, "There is a lot of drama at the office," most people immediately understand and no formal definition is necessary. However, the term has also been used in some very specific ways in academics, in psychology, in counseling and more recently in business.

This section explores the often-underestimated high cost of drama in business (and all organizational life), as well as some surprising insights about how, with practice, leaders learn to shift themselves and others out of the drama and into more productive interactions.

Drama dynamics, as they have been called by several researchers and popular authors, may involve negative feeling states such as tension, pressure, disappointment, and frustration; or they may involve counterproductive behaviors such as procrastination, blaming, or excuse making. When managers and employees get locked into these dysfunctional, self-reinforcing patterns, the ensuing tension, stress, and agitation generated can undermine individual and organizational effectiveness.

Consider for a moment what it would be like to have a drama-free workplace. Imagine how much more productive your team(s) would be if most people took responsibility for their actions, reactions, and results; if they stopped placing blame and instead supported one another in working toward shared goals, with the ability to easily resolve misunderstandings and conflicts and quickly return to productivity.

Although the following material and many of the terms may be new, the territory that this map is describing is all too familiar to the vast majority of executives who enter the Stagen Leadership

Academy. As you will see, this primer weaves together classical insights into human nature with current neuroscience and integral theory. As such, for our purposes here, we have chosen to use a classic frame that is likely familiar to all readers: being "reactive" vs. being "responsive."

These reactive interpersonal and organizational dynamics characterize what Stagen refers to as the "current level" for most leaders and their organizations.

The path to the "next level" involves the development of leadership skills that help minimize reactive patterns and maximize organizational health and performance.

Reactive Mindsets

The reactive patterns that produce drama are well understood by experts and have been described in numerous publications over several decades.

This primer will highlight some of the most helpful insights and provide practical ways that leaders can begin to apply them immediately.

One of the most well-known of these experts is bestselling author Stephen Covey. As many readers will recall, his first habit of highly effective people is "Be proactive" which he contrasts with people engaging a reactive mindset. "They find external sources to blame for their behavior. If the weather is good, they feel good. If it isn't, it affects their attitude and performance, and they blame the weather."

As Covey and so many others have counseled, when we adopt a reactive mindset, we experience life as "happening to us." This results in a lot of complaining, blaming, making excuses, and subconsciously seeking out others who validate this view. (As the old saying goes, misery loves company.)

Moving deeper into leadership and management theory, it becomes clear that much of the research in the fields of emotional intelligence in particular and adult development in general points to the lifelong process of maturing from unconscious, unresourceful "reactive" mindsets and behavior (that aggravate drama and difficulty), to more conscious, resourceful "responsive" mindsets and behavior (that lead to individual effectiveness and organizational success).

Harvard's Robert Kegan has provided a particularly useful framework. Many well-known authors, management consultants and coaches draw inspiration from his nuanced maps of how human beings develop from less mature ways of thinking and acting to progressively more mature stages. One such pioneer is Bob Anderson, the founder and CEO of The Leadership Circle. Anderson incorporated Kegan's model into his integral approach to assessing, coaching and developing leaders.

In his widely respected white paper entitled "Spirit of Leadership" Anderson explains how most people successfully make it through childhood socialization to become well-functioning, effective citizens. They take up a particular role in society and spend a significant part of their adult lives (and in some cases, the rest of their lives) conforming to that society's expectations of them. Anderson calls this stage of psychological maturity (called "level of development" in developmental psychology and integral theory) the "Reacting Stage."

As Anderson describes them, people at this stage are "defined from the outside in." They do not yet see the extent to which they are following the dictates of cultural conditioning. Developmental research shows that the vast majority of adults function at this stage and within the transition to the next stage.

Harvard's Robert Kegan talks about the fact that leaders who are driving an agenda also have an "agenda driving them." When leaders are unaware of their internal worldviews (and meaning making), especially if those beliefs and values were adopted from how they were raised (as opposed to choosing them as adults), they would be considered by developmental psychologists to be, by definition, "reactive."

Former MIT Professor Fred Kofman, author of the book *Conscious Business,* has incorporated Kegan's developmental model into his work with more than 30,000 leaders at dozens of Fortune 1000 firms. Kofman has written and spoken at length about the negative implication of this reactive mindset on individual productivity, teamwork and culture.

Psychologist Dr. Stephen Karpman has offered the most prolific and nuanced explanation of these reactive drama dynamics. He is the pioneer who first coined the term "Drama Triangle" in the early 1960s and whose groundbreaking work inspired a generation of psychologists to help their patients with a rich variety of intrapersonal and interpersonal difficulties. Karpman's unique approach using transactional and script analysis led to a rich model that posits not one but three different reactive "roles" that people play to reinforce the drama in their lives. We have found these roles to be universally familiar to people, once they understand them.

The three roles Karpman popularized and are in widespread use still today are referred to as: 1) "victim," 2) "persecutor," and 3) "rescuer."

It is important to understand that Karpman's roles, which we prefer to think of as "mindsets" are actually "orientations" and "attitudes," not personality types or stations in life. This is extremely important and can not be over-emphasized.

So when using Karpman's term "victim," it is the "role," orientation or mentality we are referring to. We are not suggesting a character trait or life circumstance. These mindset terms should never be confused with actual "victims" such as victims of violence, abuse or horrific life circumstances. The latter use of the term "victim" is a statement about life circumstances and specific life events that result in serious harm. In this training, the term victim is always used as shorthand for a "victim mindset." Please make sure that you understand and use this distinction. Especially anytime you use the term "victim" in organizational life such as with employees or co-workers.

Two other intriguing aspects of this model are worth mentioning here by way of introduction. First, these mindsets can often shift from one to another very quickly (minutes or even seconds). In fact, it is not uncommon for people to play multiple drama "roles" in a single conversation. Second, these drama patterns can become so deeply woven into the fabric of relationships that we can't even see them despite the fact that we are being negatively impacted daily by the same drama we are unwittingly creating.

The Victim Mindset

Steven Karpman dubbed the first of the three reactive minds as the "victim role" and characterizes it as feeling "persecuted" by someone or something. Victims feel that they are at the "effect" of life, rather than being the "cause" of events and circumstances. The unquestioned belief that they are always being persecuted by someone (or something) triggers an unconscious search for someone (or something) to "rescue" them. The "persecutor" could be a person or a thing such as deadlines or the economy. In this dynamic, the victim believes that they need to be "rescued" by someone or perhaps something such as the escapism that can be found through alcohol, food or television.

Employees who have adopted this victim mindset can be very frustrating for managers. They tend to blame all of their difficulties—including their own poor performance—on factors outside themselves. They strongly resist taking responsibility for their lives and circumstances; yet they excel at complaining and making excuses. You can likely think of numerous people in your work and personal life who sometimes, or often, adopt this mindset.

When people fall into this mode of thinking, they tend to feel somewhat powerless, overwhelmed or even hopeless. Clearly, high performance is rarely ever a result from this drama-drenched state of mind.

While it is true that people who are more psychologically-mature experience less drama and those at more modest stages of development experience more drama, it is important to realize that these mindsets are not characteristics of unhealthy people, deficient minds, or the psychologically compromised. Rather, we all succumb to these familiar reactive mindsets from time to time.

It is very important to accept the fact that this is not a function of whether you ever play these reactive roles in your life; rather, it is a function of how, how often and with whom.

The victim "mode," as we sometimes call it, is simply that state of mind where we feel more inclined to complain than to take responsibility for our situation and do something proactive about it. Plain and simple.

Each of these reactive mindsets telegraphs tell-tale signs of their presence in the form of specific words and phrases that you will learn to recognize. The "language" of the victim is the language of complaint. It sounds like: "This stinks." "Why is this happening to me?" "There's nothing I can do about it." Kofman cites several additional colorful examples of victim language, such as "The bus was late." "The traffic was horrendous." "My boss is an idiot." "Our IT sucks."

Stop and ask yourself, "How often do I complain?"

This includes both when you complain out loud to others and when you complain silently to yourself. Perhaps you complain about traffic, the slow-moving elevator, or the weather. Most people report that they complain so often that it's difficult to count—dozens to hundreds of times per day. An honest assessment of one's relationships—with family, coworkers, and/or boss—usually reveals that there is, in fact, a lot of complaining going on.

When you catch yourself complaining, this is a fairly reliable clue that at least in that moment, you have slipped into the victim mindset. The next time you complain, notice how this mindset feels. Does it feel energizing? Is it associated with a feeling of confidence? Does it inspire action? The answer is, of course, no. It's important to begin to recognize these subtle cues in your subjective experience. How does it feel? It feels as if life is happening to you—that you are a victim of circumstance. You are now in touch with your inner victim. But wait, in order to feel like a victim, someone or something must be acting upon us—persecuting us. That leads us to the next role in the drama dynamic.

The Persecutor Mindset

Recall that all of the mindsets that Karpman describes are reactive by nature. While the three roles he describes have different ways of reacting, they all lack awareness, resourcefulness, and conscious choice. It would be a fair statement to say that they are emotionally immature, unwise and unskillful ways to deal with life's circumstances. As such, these kinds of reactions often contribute to misunderstandings, ill feelings, and poor decisions, which in turn reinforce in ongoing, self-reinforcing cycles of dysfunction.

That's why the experts refer to these as dynamics and not merely behaviors.

The Karpman "persecutor" role is one that most employees and leaders alike play occasionally, and some habitually. This mindset is often correlated with stress—both the stress that triggers the person to act this way, and the stress of the people that have to endure the oppressive negativity that results from it. People prone to this behavior are often triggered into this mindset when they feel frustrated, threatened, defensive, or angry. Persecutors react to these emotional states by lashing out toward others with blame, harsh criticism, accusations, and controlling or dominating behavior.

Think of people you have known. Consider colleagues or managers with tendencies to get defensive, have short fuses, or frequently criticize and blame others. This is a universal experience. As with the other reactive modes, this one can be easily recognized by its language, the language of blame. "This is your fault." "Why did you do it like that?" "What's the matter with you?"

Does this language sound familiar? It should, because you undoubtedly have—at some point in your life—dealt with managers, bosses, or perhaps owners whose leadership style relied heavily on this kind of behavior.

Perhaps you have known co-workers who get frustrated when deadlines aren't met or when results are disappointing and harshly criticize or verbally attack others.

Have you ever employed this persecutor style? Perhaps more often than you would like to admit. If you ever find yourself short on patience yet long on criticism, then you are playing the role of persecutor.

Sometimes the very frustration you feel that triggers this reaction may come from growing weary of helping someone who seems incapable of helping themselves. To understand how this can happen, we will explore the rescuer mindset next.

The Rescuer Mindset

While Karpman's first two roles are fairly easy to spot and are universally viewed as undesirable, his third is a bit more nuanced and can be harder to spot. He dubbed this reactive role the "rescuer" which, at first, sounds positive. After all, rescuers help save others, right?

Not in the case of drama dynamics. In fact, this role is perhaps the most pernicious of them all precisely because it frequently goes undetected, producing harmful effects for years or even decades.

Rescuing—as we are defining the term here—is when a person shields another from the consequences of their actions. Specifically, rescuers solve victims' problems for them rather than helping them solve their own problems. As a result, the victim doesn't learn. The key issue here is that the victim's "problem" was caused (or at least contributed to) by his action or non-action. Therefore, what on the surface looks like helping behavior, is actually harmful because it prevents the person from recognizing and understanding his contribution to the problem in the first place, it short-circuits the potential learning experience, and reinforces the victim's helplessness and dependency upon someone or something to rescue him.

Here, a well-worn metaphor points to a deeper truth about human nature that even the ancients understood. Rescuing is a classic case of "giving a man a fish" instead of teaching him how to fish.

At a minimum, rescuing encourages and reinforces victim thinking and behavior. At its worst, it can produce learned helplessness in individuals or entire cultures. These are serious implications for leaders to consider

Earlier, we used the example of victims in a burning building being rescued by brave firefighters. Ironically, that is not far from how people who identify with this mindset actually see themselves: as heroes. Karpman's chosen term for this role underscores the justification that people use for this particular drama dynamic (namely, that the victim needs rescuing).

Each mindset has specific words and phrases that indicate it. The language of the rescuer is the language of fixing. Examples include: "I feel sorry for you." "Let me help you." "I'll just do it myself."

It is important to realize that rescuers are well meaning, and in most cases, are genuinely unaware of their harmful effects.

"But I only wanted to help!"

Despite their good intentions, by giving people answers or fixing their problems for them, the rescuer is inadvertently blocking the other person's opportunity to learn and develop. Perhaps more concerning is the fact that most rescuers have an ulterior motive, which is rarely acknowledged, and is often unconscious.

Think about rescuers you have known and consider, what is the "payoff" for this behavior? The payoff is that rescuers get to feel like heroes—needed, important, right, or even superior.

Recall that the dynamism in Karpman's Drama Triangle comes from the fact that the three drama roles are in continual reaction to one another. The action of one triggers a reaction in the next, which in turn produces an unconscious response like a "domino effect." The victim needs a perceived persecutor (person or thing) so that they don't have to take responsibility for their lives. Since victims see themselves at the mercy of circumstances, overwhelmed, incapable or even helpless, they need help! A struggling victim is irresistible to a rescuer who is more than happy to play that role, and in the process, satisfy their need to feel needed.

We can characterize development in the team (interpersonal) dimension as going from "compliance" to "collaboration." As such, the persecutor can be seen to demand compliance, the victim helplessly complies, and the rescuer can be thought of as helping (rationalizing) the victim's compliance with (acceptance of) the conditions that are persecuting the "victim."

It gets really interesting when one individual plays all three roles in the drama, or shifts from one role to another, such as the persecutor shifting into a victim mindset when the results of their persecuting behavior offend them in some way.

Can you think of a time when you put on a "one man" or "one woman" show? Try to remember a time that you felt sorry for yourself because circumstances were not in your favor and so your performance was disappointing? (This is you in the role of the victim who needs rescuing.)

Perhaps you then beat yourself up with the harsh voice of the inner critic for not finding a way to turn in a better performance. (This is you in the role of the persecutor.) Perhaps then, you indulged in coping behaviors such as eating or drinking too much. (This is you rescuing yourself). Finally, recognizing your indulgence, you feel terrible, and at that moment, a little bit hopeless. (Emotionally exhausted, you return back to the victim).

You may have noticed that you are more inclined to some roles than others. This is true of everyone. People who tend to make excuses and feel helpless gravitate toward the victim role. People with an inclination for impatience, blame or criticism tend toward the persecutor role. Finally, people whose self-esteem is identified with being smart, helpful, and/or having the answers can tend toward the rescuer mindset.

Escaping the drama triangle requires us to accurately recognize these roles we play with ourselves, our teams, our employees, and our families. While this can be, initially, slightly humbling, it is in fact the beginning of the process of learning to avoid and/or minimize drama in our offices and our homes.

The High Cost of Drama in Organizational Life

It should be becoming clear that this exploration of drama is more than an indulgence into the "soft skills" of leadership. In fact, precisely the opposite is true. These deeply dysfunctional and productivity-draining mindsets, behaviors, and social system dynamics are more than an annoyance. If you are like most leaders who have come through the Stagen Leadership Academy, these stress-inducing, energy-sapping, morale-draining, productivity-destroying habits may be a major reason why you are not yet enjoying the success you are so committed to in your business. Moreover, these habits can cause strained relationships and missed opportunities for connection and happiness at home.

Numerous authors have written about the impact of trust on organizational performance. Patrick Lencioni, author of The Five Dysfunctions of a Team, suggests that trust is the foundation of high performance teamwork. Others have suggested that trust is the social glue that holds a company together. Drama erodes trust as fast as anything we've seen. Do not underestimate the high cost of drama.

Awareness is half the solution. As such, we have found that when leaders grasp the actual neurological and psychological mechanics of drama, it accelerates their ability to sidestep those old habits and rewire their mental circuits with new thinking and behavior resulting in immediate improvements in their leadership performance.

Drama on the Brain

Perhaps it is simply part of human nature that people want to point outside themselves to what seem to be the sources of drama in their lives. However, as shown in the previous section, it is more accurate to say that the drama is an "inside job."

A brief review of the brain's structure offers leaders insights into the biological source of drama and surprisingly effective ways to sidestep it. As you likely already know, humans actually have three brains—or more precisely, three brain sections—each serving very different functions.

The brain stem area is referred to as the "lower brain," or the "reptilian brain" (because humans share this structure with reptiles). This part of the brain generates self-protective responses that aid physical survival, such as blinking, flinching, and other reflexes; and it monitors and influences many essential autonomic bodily functions, such as breathing and digesting food. It is responsible for territoriality, aggression, and other reptile-like behaviors.

The "middle brain" is also referred to as the "limbic" or "mammalian" brain and includes the amygdala (made famous by Emotional Intelligence pioneer Dr. Daniel Goleman's concept of "Amygdala Hijacking"). The limbic system (brain) is responsible for social and nurturing behaviors, mutual reciprocity, and other behaviors that humans share with other mammals. Mammals require this structure because, unlike reptiles, they are not merely laying eggs and leaving them, but rather are raising offspring, hunting together, and needing to coordinate numerous group activities to live together successfully.

It is this same brain capacity that allows humans to collect a lot of unconscious information about what other people are feeling. The brain's mirror neurons allow people to quickly recognize the feelings of another just by seeing their facial expression and hearing the tone of their voice (also known as empathy). In order to be highly effective, leaders need to be aware of other people's mental and emotional states. These capacities are made possible by the functions of the limbic brain.

Finally, the highest, newest, and most complex part of the brain is the neocortex. The neocortex is responsible for functions such as reason, strategic thinking, planning, and mental simulation (also known as "perspective-taking"). This is the "highest brain" because it literally sits atop the other two; and once adequately trained, it can actually guide and direct the other two brains with great dexterity. Daniel Goleman refers to this phenomenon as "self mastery," which has everything to do with self-awareness, recognizing emotional triggers, and managing one's own mental and emotional states for maximum enjoyment, effectiveness, and potency as a human being.

Who's Really in Charge?

When people allow our reptilian or mammalian brain to simply react, the results tend to fall into various shades of fight (aggressive or defensive) or flight (avoidance).

You can no doubt think of people in your life, perhaps coworkers, who are easily triggered into feelings of frustration, anger, or defensiveness when circumstances don't go their way. These kinds of amygdala hijackings result in otherwise well-intentioned people saying and doing things that they later regret. In these kinds of reactive situations, it is often these instinctive brain functions that are "driving the bus."

So who is in charge in your own life? Are you the one "driving your bus?" Are you sure?

Emotionally mature leaders who are skillful and effective in their interpersonal dealings remain calm and effective even under the pressure of missed deadlines, frustrating disappointments, and even verbal attacks. In brain terms, these leaders have learned how to utilize their neocortex to steer their mammalian and reptilian brain functions. As masters of their lower brains, they are now able to catch and stop emotional reactions before they hijack their nervous system. They can even learn to transform negative emotional energy into care, concern, commitment, drive, or if necessary, assertiveness. Rather than reacting to life's circumstances, leaders firmly at the helm of their neocortex are able to make conscious choices about how to respond wisely and skillfully.

In a very real sense, conscious leaders use their neocortex to "steer" their reptilian and mammalian brain functions. Indeed, mature leaders can learn to drive their own neurological bus rather than turn the control of their nervous system into the hands of random people who may not even have their best interests in mind.

Richard Bandler, the pioneering and controversial co-founder of the pop psychology field called "Neuro-Linguistic Programming" was fond of saying, "Who's driving the bus?"

We would suggest that climbing into the driver's seat of your brain is job number one for leaders who are serious about improving their relationships, their job performance, and the success of their organization.

As a proactive, responsive and creative leader, you can take deliberate steps to train yourself to take a deliberate pause between stimulus and response.

By taking a moment to engage your neocortex for perspective taking, reasoning, and analysis, you can begin to discern between more probable and less probable scenarios, generate many additional possibilities of what might actually be happening, and render a higher definition, more accurate mental picture of what is really happening in a given circumstance.

In another lesson, we provide a specific technique I developed at Integral Institute and became very popular at the leadership academy I co-founded in the early 2000s called Stagen Leadership Academy. It is called "Recalibration" and uses three steps to help leaders re-condition their mind and nervous system to "stop," "ground" and then "center."

Responsive Mindsets

Making the shift from a current-level leader to a next-level leader involves more than simply learning a few verbal techniques to avoid conflict, if only it were that easy. In order to meaningfully upgrade your leadership capacity, you must develop and strengthen your social and emotional intelligence capacities, and in the process, internalize new cognitive, verbal and behavioral skills.

The developmental experts introduced earlier (Anderson, Kofman, and Kegan), offer compelling arguments for the benefit of moving from reactive to responsive modes.

To fully and permanently escape the Drama Triangle, people must learn to consciously choose their own thinking, values, beliefs, and deliberate responses to life circumstances. The practices introduced in this section are designed to strengthen the very capacities that leaders require to successfully get to their "next level."

The practice we call "Escaping the Drama Triangle" involves building a kind of developmental scaffolding that helps us learn how to take responsibility, be creative, and skillfully coach and challenge others to achieve better results. By adopting and ultimately internalizing these new habits, we rewire our brains' mental and emotional circuits. In time, we behave less and less like emotionally immature adolescents and more like the consistently mature leaders we aspire to become.

Bob Anderson characterizes this process as the major transition of adult life. He points out that only an estimated 20% of adults fully complete this journey to self-authorship. Anderson points out that in order to become fully "Creative" (his term for self-authoring), "We face the fact that following our own path often means disappointing others, risking failure, and/or otherwise contradicting the norms that link me to society... This transition is particularly difficult because, to make this journey, I have to let go of how I have come to define myself. I let go of the deeply held beliefs that my worth and value are tied up with what I do. I am no longer defined by cultural expectations."

Anderson and many other researchers have described leaders who have matured to the "Creative" or self-authoring stage. Jim Collins calls them "Level Five Leaders."

John Mackey, founder of Whole Foods and author of *Conscious Capitalism: Liberating the Heroic Spirit of Business*, describes them as "conscious leaders."

Bill George, founder of Medtronic and author of *True North: Discover Your Authentic Leadership,* refers to self-authoring leaders as "authentic leaders."

Bill Torbert, Boston College's School of Management professor and co-author of the popular Harvard Business Review article "The Seven Transformations of Leadership" calls them "Individualists."

Well over two decades of experience advising, mentoring, training and coaching leaders has shown us that leaders who complete the climb from their current level (of psychological maturity) to the next must be willing to adopt new ways of thinking and acting.

If you are curious about what it's like to be a "self-authoring leader," Anderson offers a compelling description…

"Now, I configure a self from the inside out for the first time. Vision springs from within. Action becomes an authentic expression of an emerging sense of inner purpose. As I begin to see and experience the power, creativity, freedom, and satisfaction of living from my own deep center, I also value and encourage that in others. I begin to treat others as equal participating members, whose rights, insights, and purposes need to be engaged and creatively aligned. Self-expression and cooperation become our new organizing principles."

Introducing David Emerald's "Empowerment Dynamic"

Hopefully, at this point, you are ready to take concrete steps toward becoming a more responsive leader. Here is the good news: Despite all the unnecessary stress and cost of drama in our workplace, once we learn to accurately identify the drama mindsets, they offer very specific clues as to how we can respond consciously and creatively—in a way that is more consistent with psychologically-mature, self-authoring adults. Thanks to the pioneering work of our colleague David Emerald (who has also worked extensively with Bob Anderson), leaders can actually use the drama mindsets as stepping-stones toward what he calls the "Empowerment Dynamic."

My colleagues and I are committed to helping leaders accelerate their own development toward greater maturity, potency, and power as effective leaders. Representing a kind of developmental scaffolding, maps and methodologies can help leaders quickly evaluate situations and then rapidly respond with optimal approaches. Emerald's Empowerment Dynamic is one of the effective tools in our leadership development toolkit.

Working closely with Bob Anderson's organization, Emerald was interested in finding an effective alternative to Karpman's three drama mindsets (victim, persecutor, challenger). He certainly succeeded. His model is explained in his book, *The Power of T.E.D.,* and elaborated upon in many articles, publications, and extensive workshops he has offered. Emerald's approach provides a powerful and practical set of tools that conscious leaders can use to transform drama-filled workplaces into productive, highly-engaged organizations. One of the most helpful features of David Emerald's "Empowerment Dynamic" framework is the simplicity of his precise one-to-one ratio: the "victim" reaction is replaced by what he calls a "creator" response. The "persecutor" reaction is replaced with the "challenger" response.

The persecutor approach is replaced by a "challenger" mindset. And thirdly, the rescuer mentality shifts into a "coach" orientation. You don't have to be a leadership theorist to recognize that two of the most common "roles" that effective leaders must play are to be "coaches" and "challengers" to their followers.

The "Creator" Mindset

As people develop from less mature stages characterized by a pervasive victim mentality rife with excuse-making and blaming others—into more mature stages, their experience of life and relationships becomes more consistently characterized by a sense of personal responsibility, interpersonal accord, and skillful action. In short, more psychologically-mature leaders, teams, and workers result in less workplace drama.

Psychologically mature people, and that certainly includes leaders, respond to life circumstances and the people in their lives in a way that is more measured, more thoughtful, more emotionally balanced, more skillful, and, frankly, more helpful. Isn't this true in your own experience? Think of your productive and mature employees. Their lives, relationships, and work are often characterized by less drama, less stress, and, as Covey has so well pointed out, more "effectiveness."

Previously, the victim mindset was characterized by complaints, excuses, and a refusal to take responsibility. By contrast, the shift to the creator mindset is characterized by a willingness to accept responsibility, take initiative, and make creative choices.

When we are identified with what Emerald calls a "creator" mindset and we can refer to it as a "responsive" mindset, people tend to feel more capable, confident, resourceful, and emotionally resilient.

Emerald chose the word "creator" as the name of this mindset for very specific reasons. When in victim mode, people feel as though they are at the effect of life.

In this case, people are reacting to life's circumstances (often instinctively and with little awareness, much less creativity). Emerald describes that when people shift into the creator mode, they consciously choose their responses to their life circumstances.

As effective as you are as a leader, you can never fully control external circumstances (i.e., your employees' attitudes and behaviors, your customers' choices, or the economy). But if you are conscious, you can certainly choose how you respond (mentally, emotionally, and behaviorally) to those external circumstances. Every experience and interaction offers you the opportunity to choose a creative, intelligent response.

The mental and emotional shift from victim to creator amounts to a re-orientation whereby one responds resourcefully to people and circumstances rather than reacting un-resourcefully.

You will recall the language of the victim is the language of complaint. By contrast, the language of the creator is the language of commitment. Examples include: "The outcome I'm going to create is…," "The learning I'm getting from this is…", "I choose to…"

Faced with disappointment or frustration, the victim feels sorry for himself and complains. In contrast, the creator accepts the reality that these are the circumstances he is in, and takes responsibility for responding in a way that is helpful and productive. In short, the creator accepts responsibility for "creating a response" that has a better chance of moving him toward his desired outcome than merely complaining or making excuses. As managers, we see examples of victim responses and examples of creator responses daily both in ourselves and from our colleagues and employees.

Challenger Mindset

While the corollary to the victim mindset is the creator, the corollary to the persecutor mindset is the challenger.

When you shift into the challenger mindset, you evoke or provoke the "will to create" in others. Challengers tend to feel clear, confident, centered and committed. The language of the challenger is the language of change. Examples include: "I believe you can do better than this." "You need to come back when you have a solution to this." "You have to take a different approach."

Sports dads can offer inspiration for leaders learning to be more consistent challengers. A father who believes in his child's potential evokes or, if necessary, provokes her desire to improve, work harder, and achieve goals. On the other hand, you may have witnessed sports dads (or moms, for that matter) who may be well-intentioned, but instead of building their kids up, they employ blame and criticism that can erode the child's self-esteem.

Leaders can take a cue from the playbook of those "sports dads" who are effective challengers. As a leader who believes in the potential of your employees, you can assertively remind them that they are capable of more, and you can insist that he raise his "game" in order to meet the job requirements. The main difference between persecuting and challenging is that even though both use an assertive tone, the former has the intention and effect of "tearing down," while the latter has both the intention and effect of "building up." The next time you feel frustrated or disappointed and are tempted to persecute, ask yourself, "What is my intention?" If your intention is to motivate the person to do better, then try challenging rather than persecuting.

Coach Mindset

You will recall that someone in the rescuer mindset shields others from the consequences of their actions and short-circuits their ability to learn from experience (especially mistakes). Emerald's coaching mindset is an extremely potent antidote to that mentality. To revisit our handy fish analogy, rescuers give fish, coaches teach people how to fish.

When you adopt the coach mindset, you support others in tapping into their own innate capabilities to solve problems, get better results, or learn to do something for themselves (so that they no longer act like a victim).

The language of coaching is the language of questioning. Examples of questions that coaches ask include: "What is that you really want?", "What do you see as your options?", "What can you choose to do to improve this situation?"

Contrast this with the language of rescuing: fixing. Whereas rescuers give people answers (or solve the other person's problem for them), a coach asks questions.

When you have adopted this mindset, you tend to feel supportive, optimistic, and non-attached to the outcome.

This term "non-attached" is new to some readers. Non-attached is a psychological term that refers to your recognition that you are fundamentally okay if you don't achieve your desired outcome (or the person you are coaching doesn't achieve hers/his). Sure, you might be disappointed or even frustrated if you don't get "your way", but you are psychologically stable enough that you are not rattled to your core when the reality of life doesn't match up with your expectations about it.

Being emotionally non-attached does not mean that you don't care. Of course, you care and you have your preferences; however, you realize that your basic health and safety, self-worth, or emotional peace of mind are not threatened just because a situation doesn't unfold according to your preferences.

Non-attachment is one of the key qualities of the coach mindset for a very important reason: if you can't remain emotionally non-attached to the other person's outcome, then you are in the drama triangle with them.

Being a coach requires you to allow the other person to retain full responsibility for their behavior and their outcome.

Recall that the language of the rescuer is the language of fixing. Contrast this with the language of the coach, which is the language of questions. Coaches ask questions designed to help the person shift out from victim mode, and instead, learn from experience and solve their own problems.

A few examples of the type of questions that coaches ask include: "What is it you really want?", "What do you see as your options?", "What were you trying to achieve?", "What can you do to improve the situation next time?"

Coaching and Challenging is an Investment Into Your Employees and Team

Of course, it takes longer in the short run to be a coach rather than a rescuer, and a challenger rather than a persecutor. However, it is far more effective in the long run to have competent, engaged, and well-trained employees who take initiative and who are continually learning and growing in their jobs and careers.

Challenging, in particular, can feel somewhat counterintuitive, especially when you are annoyed with the person's lack of results, or worse, lack of effort. How do you positively "build up" someone with whom you are disappointed? The answer lies in your mindset. You must be willing to envision the person as having the potential to do better, even if they have not previously lived up to that potential.

David Emerald suggests that you must see the victim as having the potential to be a creator. Why? Because if you continue to see them as incompetent or lazy, then you will likely want to criticize or blame (persecute). To evoke the desire to do better, you must be willing to see them as actually having potential. Then, instead of blaming or criticizing them, you tell them, "I know you can do better than this. You must step up your game if you are to stay on this team." Or, "I believe that you can do this, and I'm willing to support you; but you must show me a higher level of commitment and effort than I've seen up until now."

Caution Against "Leading Under the Influence"

Reactive leaders sow the seeds of drama and dysfunction in their organizations. Anytime you indulge in reactive thinking and behavior, you are eroding trust, credibility, and morale. It is very important to become aware of your emotional triggers and to have the presence of mind to avoid leading under the influence of them.

Now that you are familiar with the reactive mindsets that create drama, and the more three resourceful responsive mindsets, you have the opportunity and responsibility to choose how you want to lead.

Recall the discussion earlier about the brain. When you become emotionally triggered (feeling threatened, defensive, anxious, angry, or aggressive), your amygdala takes over and moves your brain and body into fight-or-flight mode. In a very real way—both biologically and anatomically—you are now in a compromised mental state.

This state is referred to as being "emotionally flooded." In other words, there is a neurological "brown-out" in the cortical centers of the brain that govern many of the higher brain functions associated with reason, empathy, perspective-taking, and abstract thinking. Being under the influence of negative emotions is a lot like being under the influence of drugs or alcohol.

As a responsible adult, you avoid driving "under the influence." Then why, we ask, would you lead under the influence of negative emotions?

Like alcoholics, drama addicts are so accustomed to stress, blame, criticism, and excuse-making that they become numb and unaware that they are "intoxicated" by negative emotions. However, like with drunk driving, ignorance is not a valid excuse. It is reckless behavior to lead while under the influence of being emotionally triggered. Don't do it.

The Power of Managing Our Attention

For the past 23 years, I have written and taught extensively about attention. One of our most popular trainings at the Stagen Leadership Academy is called "Attention Management." I include versions of that training (which has evolved over the last two decades as media and culture has evolved) in my book in this series, *Execution & Performance*. This topic of "attention" bears special emphasis here in this section on organizational drama. Over the last two decades, cognitive science has validated what wise teachers have counseled for generations: if you change the focus of your attention, you can change how you feel, and even what things mean (interpretations). Shifting attention changes our neurophysiological state which can immediately, and positively impact performance. This insight has been successfully applied in the military, sports, psychotherapy, medicine, and now management.

David Emerald (the author of The Power of T.E.D.) reminds us that our Focus (conception) influences our Inner State (emotion), which in turn influences our Behavior (actions). He introduced the acronym "FISBE" to help us remember this. Our focus influences our inner state which in turn influences our behavior. His model highlights the two alternative ways this dynamic can unfold: a vicious cycle created by the "victim" mindset or as a virtuous cycle cultivated by a "creator" mindset.

Starting with the vicious cycle, the victim's narrow focus on the problem produces an inner state of anxiety, which causes him to react. This reaction often exacerbates the problem, reinforcing the cycle. In the virtuous cycle, the creator focuses on his vision for what he wants or the outcome he is trying to achieve. This influences his inner state to feel more feelings of passion, excitement, or commitment. This inner state influences behavior by motivating the creator to take a step in the direction of his desired outcome. Even a small amount of forward progress further reinforces the virtuous cycle.

We have taught this model to thousands of leaders over the last two decades. This experience has shown us that the momentum of the victim's vicious cycle can be reversed with a single question: "What do I really want?" Variations include: What do I want? What do I want to happen here? What do we want as a team? What do we want as an organization? As a coach, you can ask others these questions.

With practice, people begin to realize how much control they have over their own cybernetic system. They recognize that they do not have to be such "victims of circumstance" if they choose not to be.

As mature, effective, integrally-informed leaders, instead of reacting instinctively, we take responsibility for our thoughts, our emotional reactions, and our behaviors. By choosing deliberately what we're going to focus on, how we focus on it, and the meaning we make of it, we can now —in a very real sense—leverage our power to respond.

Gamefilming Drama as a Reflective Practice to Accelerate Learning

We recommend that leaders begin the "Escaping the Drama Triangle" practice in a basic way, and the more you practice deliberately and mindfully, the more you see the possibilities and the potential. Start in your own backyard, so to speak, with your own mind and reactions. Catch yourself complaining, making excuses, and blaming.

My good friend Rand Stagen (my co-founder of the Stagen Leadership Academy) built out an idea I had to draw on a sports analogy and refer to contemplation, self-observation, and what "making subject object" as "Gamefilming." You are no doubt familiar that professional athletes film themselves then review that film to learn about their performance (and to improve it). Rand and I took that metaphor pretty far in our work training executives in our the *Integral Leadership Program*.

This metaphor is a really useful one, and one I encourage you to adopt. The term "gamefilming," as my colleagues and I use it, refers to a deliberate practice of self-observation that accelerates learning and drives successful performance. While my colleagues and I have developed many "gamefilming" methods, one of the simplest and most effective is keeping a log of specific interactions and behaviors that relate to the skill you are learning. As you gamefilm your own drama, important issues in your work and home life will surface as themes, patterns, and (emotional) triggers. A log will help you capture, track, and analyze these high-leverage dynamics. Address these issues, and you will be surprised at how quickly your leadership performance improves.

Some practitioners initially resist putting down their raw thoughts that pop into their heads. Perhaps they are a little bit embarrassed to specify those thoughts about that colleague, customer or spouse. But if you are serious about your development, then you must have the courage to watch the "game film." Put another way, it's crucial to have an honest assessment when you look into that mirror. After all, these are your thoughts and reactions. These are the behaviors of your mind, your neurology. Specificity gives us developmental traction. Alas, integral leadership development is not for cowards or the fainthearted.

Day after day, week after week, as you become familiar with how these interpersonal and psychological principles and practices work, you have a better understanding of what's also happening for other people.

It should now be clear that we are not merely talking about what some call "soft skills"—as if emotional and interpersonal dynamics are less valuable than the hard business skills of finance, operations, and strategy. As we have seen, every one of the people in your organization is subject to the influence of the three parts of the human brain. People are frequently working under the influence of negative emotions and reactive mindsets. As such, everyone working in your organization is either helped or hindered by the presence or absence of drama.

Please recall that these new attitudes and skills take time to learn, practice and internalize—not days or weeks, but months and years. The good news is that by applying what you have learned in this primer, you will see an immediate improvement in communication, cooperation, and results. The even better news is that after a few months of deliberate practice, people who know you will likely begin to offer you feedback on how much easier you are to work with (or live with) and how much more effective you are becoming as a leader. In time, they may even report how much more enjoyable it is to work in such a positive, empowered, low-drama environment.

In this chapter we covered the benchmarks and some of the most important frameworks, practices, techniques and tools that the most successful leaders use to bolster the "Creating the Container" skill set.

Now we move to the next skill set that successful leaders use. I call this skill set, "Conscious Communication."

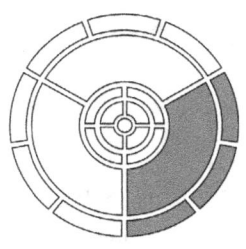

CHAPTER 7: COMMUNICATION

I am beginning each chapter on the three skill sets found in the essential ability of "Teamwork & Culture" by offering precise benchmarks so that you can evaluate your leadership and your team and pinpoint areas for improvement. I define Communication this way. Effective leadership Communication is concerned with effective communication involving social awareness, listening, framing, feedback, dialog, collaboration, working with assumptions and interpretations, and managing conflict.

Team Discussion

Use these questions to discuss this skill set with your team members.

- How do we approach communication activities such as listening, framing, and feedback?

- How do we dialog and collaborate as a team?

- How do we manage assumptions and interpretations?

- How do we handle conflict?

Benchmarks

Now we move into the benchmarks for this skill set following the same convention we used for the last skill set.

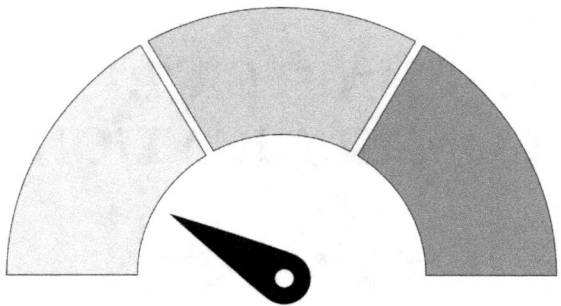

COMMUNICATION LOWER RANGE

A leader and a team functioning in the lower range of proficiency in this skill set might describe it this way.

Few of our team members have had the benefit of communication training (in things like framing, feedback, listening, dialog or conflict management). Some are naturally good communicators, but many are frankly pretty "rough around the edges." This often results in miscommunication, misunderstanding and conflict that isn't managed very well.

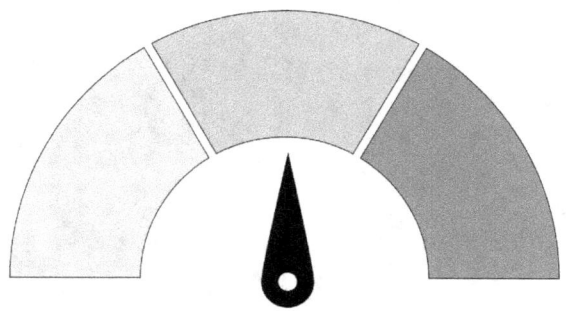

COMMUNICATION MIDDLE RANGE

A leader and a team functioning in the middle range of proficiency in this skill set might describe it this way.

Some members are good listeners who can also dialog and collaborate, but for others, communication often seems forced or strained. As an organization, we appreciate good communication, but we don't have many shared "best practices" in terms of how we use framing, feedback, listening, dialog, working with assumptions and interpretations and so on.

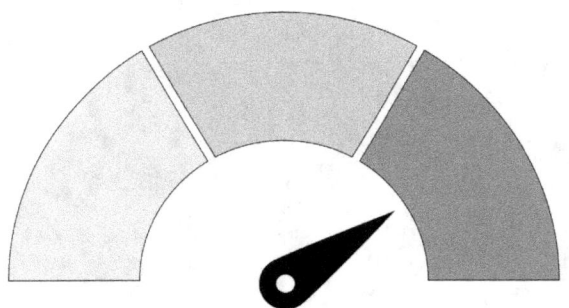

COMMUNICATION HIGHER RANGE

A leader and a team functioning in the higher range of proficiency in this skill set might describe it this way.

Overall, we have excellent communication skills. We often disagree, but we find that these disagreements actually lead to a deeper understanding of issues, and ultimately to better decision making. Most of our members are pretty good or even excellent at things like framing, feedback, listening, dialog, and handling differences of opinion and conflict.

Now that we have reviewed the benchmarks for this skill set, we will move into a detailed discussion of some of the most important "skills." It is important to think of these "skills" that make up the "skill set" as practices. It is correct to think of practices as techniques that you repeat, memorize and ultimately internalize. As I have explained elsewhere, techniques (approached as practices) over time become habit. Habits become skills. Eventually, skills weave to together into "skill sets." Finally, the skill sets come together to create an "ability." As I have stated before, think about the skills of throwing, catching, hitting and running as necessary prerequisites for the ability we call playing baseball. And of course, dribbling, passing, shooting and rebounding are the well-known skills one needs to develop the ability we call playing basketball.

Our first communication skill is to distinguish "impact" from "intent" in our communication and to learn to "adjust our aim" so that our messages more frequently "land" on the target and have the impact we intend.

Intent vs. Impact

Organizational life is rife with misunderstandings, missed opportunities, mistakes, and conflict. Many of these issues result from confusing a person's communication intent with the actual impact.

Understanding the dynamic process that occurs from intent (which happens
before the communication) through impact (which happens after the communication) can significantly enhance a leader's ability to motivate and influence effectively.

A visual analogy of an archer and a target is helpful here.

The Intent

In this analogy, the archer represents communication intent. He intends to communicate meaning to another person (or group).

MESSAGE Unfortunately, intentions (thoughts) cannot be transferred directly from one mind to another. The communicator must use words and symbols (signifiers and syntax discussed in the previous section), to convey a message as skillfully as he is able, that will closely approximate his intended meaning. The arrow represents the message, or what is actually said.

The Impact

The target represents the impact of the message on the receiver—in other words, how the message is heard and interpreted. In the unlikely case that the receiver hears and interprets the message exactly as the sender intended it, then the metaphorical target has been hit in the center of the bullseye.

Of course, this rarely happens. In the illustration, the archer's arrows are hitting the outer rings of the target, indicating that the person receiving the message is interpreting it differently than the sender intended to. Why is there so often a difference between intent and impact?

Bearing in mind all of the distinctions introduced in the previous sections of this manifesto, I would suggest that leader-follower communication often misses the mark for two fundamental reasons:

1. The "sender" lacks the skills to articulate a message that precisely reflects his or her thoughts

or;

2. The "receiver" hears/understands the message differently than the sender intended due to subjective interpretive filters (that the sender has failed to adequately adjust for).

The various communication practices introduced in this book can dramatically increase a manager's ability to hit the center of the metaphorical target.

Next, an effective leader must understand when to use each of the different modes of communication available. Further, to be an effective communicator, you must cultivate greater versatility so that you can deploy the best mode for each unique situation.

Modes of Communication

Have you considered how much is at stake when communicating with your colleagues?

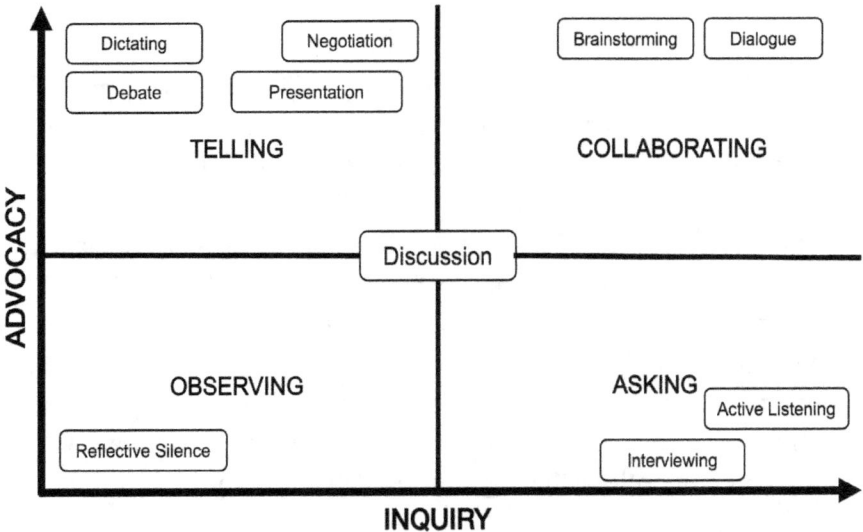

While some leaders can intuit the best mode of communication to use in different situations, this is a topic not widely taught in management training or on-the-job leadership training. There are numerous "Modes of Communication" as we will call them. I will refer to this diagram several times in this section. Take a look at the ten "modes" in this illustration.

One of the first things you may notice is your own preference for certain modes. Which of these ten listed "modes" do you gravitate toward? Which modes do you use the most? Which modes do you use very infrequently?

Which modes do you enjoy and feel confident using? Which modes are you reluctant to use or perhaps you feel less confident using?

Perhaps you are a team player who is really fond of brainstorming and dialog?

Or perhaps you are a highly directive manager who likes to just get straight to the point and let the other person know what they need to do next?

You can also think of your colleagues. Clearly, some are great observers and listeners, and others... Well, let's just say they are "enthusiastic advocates" of their own point of view.

Next, I want you to look more closely at my modes of communication X-Y diagram. I have "Advocacy" (also known as "Telling" on the vertical and "Inquiry" (also known as "Asking") on the horizontal. This creates a familiar X-Y with four quadrants (low, low, low, high, high low, high high). I label these quadrants, Telling, Asking, Collaborating and Observing respectively. I'm sure you can follow the logic here. This kind of analysis can be really helpful (and you won't find this anywhere else outside of my books and my trainings). Let's look more closely at this idea of "advocacy" (on the vertical axis). Most managers are trained to be "advocates"—to assert a point of view, debate, and influence—in an attempt to solve problems and achieve goals. But as they move into senior positions and confront more complex and diverse issues, advocacy that is not balanced with inquiry becomes problematic.

High advocacy can polarize communication with limited possible outcomes. Either person A may win, or person B may win, or both may walk away with their views unchanged (and may not feel very good about the interaction). Most people communicate habitually—completely unaware of the broad range of choices available to them. In fact, most people use only one or two modes of communication (e.g., discussion and debate) and do not take advantage of the full range of communication modes available.

Different circumstances call for different approaches to communication. People with greater awareness of a situation and a variety of modes to choose from bring greater versatility to communication and can achieve significantly better outcomes.

While this simplified chart plots only ten common modes of communication, of course there are other modes. In this chapter, I will emphasize six of the most common modes successful leaders in my training programs have found very useful in their day to day work environment. I feel confident this will apply to your situation as well.

Negotiation

Negotiation (high advocacy, low-to-medium inquiry) is rarely the first tool to reach for during most interactions. However, in situations where conflict has been building and trust is low, this highly structured mode of communication can prove extremely effective. It requires two or more parties who are willing to compromise in order to resolve a difficult dispute. The goal of this mode of communication is a durable agreement between the parties.

Presentation

This mode (medium-to-high advocacy, low inquiry) is useful in situations where one person (or a panel) is engaged in primarily one-way communication such as giving a speech, presenting a scripted proposal, or conveying the results of a research study. This has been a dominant mode of communication in business for several decades. Conscious communicators are aware of the unilateral nature of this mode and consider additional approaches as a compliment where appropriate (Q&A, asking questions of the audience, soliciting post-presentation written feedback, etc.).

Discussion

This mode (medium advocacy, medium inquiry) is useful in situations where the goal is to consider various points of view leading to a more informed decision. Though it obviously involves more two-way communication than presentation, it does not assume that everyone communicates inclusively or equally. Some people dominate, while others may not speak at all. Unfortunately, the term "discussion" can be a misnomer. Many autocratic/authoritarian style managers call for a discussion to simply hear the opposing views so that they can squash them. Or they may give the impression that other perspectives are being considered but intend to go ahead with their agendas regardless.

Active Listening

Though most readers are quick to recognize listening as an important mode of communication, few people have received active listening training or demonstrate high levels of competency with this mode of communication. Active listeners are capable of temporarily setting their agendas aside in order to understand the deeper meaning behind the speaker's message.

An active listening mindset involves:

1. Giving undivided attention (presence).

2. Listening non-judgmentally (without deciding).

3. Avoiding listening autobiographically (needing to jump in and talk about yourself).

I like to highlight five active listening techniques that are very helpful.

1. Make inquiries using open-ended questions.

2. Reflection involving paraphrasing or restating.

3. Empathizing with others' feelings and experiences.

4. Asking clarifying questions.

5. Summarizing key themes before moving to the next topic of conversation.

Dialogue

This mode (high advocacy, high inquiry) seeks to get all relevant views out into the open in order to facilitate shared understanding of the issue. Dialogue is especially useful in situations where complex and/or difficult business issues need to be considered from multiple vantage points.

Derived from the Greek *dialegesthai*, also known as "dialectical communication." It meant to speak about something in a way that the participants come to a new understanding. Dialogue implies a reciprocal, mutually-enriching communication interaction.

The main difference between discussion and dialogue is that in the latter, parties willingly set their agendas aside, suspend their interpretations and judgments, and engage in active listening for the purpose of uncovering deeper issues that might otherwise not surface. Dialogue requires that both parties feel heard and understood. Because this mode is more disarming and revealing, it generally requires more trust than other modes.

Reflective Silence

This mode (no advocacy, no inquiry) is perhaps the least used, yet one of the most powerful when used skillfully. Silence is useful because it gives people an opportunity to think about the topic without having to simultaneously follow one or more conversations. Some personality types (extroverts) think and analyze best during the heat of discussion. Other types (introverts) prefer to gather their thoughts internally and quietly before offering their concerns or ideas to the group. With a few moments of strategically placed silence, the group may be able to benefit from the ideas of the less outspoken members. Also, silence is useful because it can help shift the focus or tone of a meeting. It can serve as a bookend or segue from one phase of the conversation to another. Silence can also be used to invite conversation participants to reflect on their own assumptions, intentions, and/or interpretations.

Bring More Awareness to Your Interactions

There are three quick, easy ways to improve your communication and bring more awareness and skill to your interactions.

1. Always put inquiry before advocacy. Ask a question and be genuinely interested in the response; ask related clarifying follow-up questions BEFORE you launch into your opinions or recommendations.

2. Notice your own tendency to argue or debate your position. That "Debate" mode of communication is often overused. In most cases, you are on the same team as the people you are communicating

with. Collaborating modes tend to work better than telling modes in most cultures.

3. Don't overuse collaboration. There is a time and a place where it's useful to just get straight to the point and let the other person know their best next steps.

With awareness, you get a choice. The whole point of this exercise is to grow your capacity for awareness of which mode of communication will work best in which situations and to choose the right one that will increase your leadership versatility.

The next skill is not even remotely optional. Leaders who are effective at communication (and teamwork more broadly) must be excellent at giving feedback. There is no room for you to avoid feedback or give it using incorrect form. That is just too costly. If you are to be an adequate communicator in your role of leader, you must become proficient at giving feedback the right way.

Feedback

Feedback is a critical part of organizational life, so it is safe to say that learning and improvement are next to impossible without it. Yet, most employees surveyed in typical companies report that they do not receive all the feedback that they need to do their jobs well, much less the feedback that would help them continually improve their performance so that they can excel in their role.

And if you talk to a typical manager / executive leader, they will likely tell you that they feel uncomfortable providing necessary feedback and often procrastinates or avoids giving feedback altogether.

How would you evaluate your feedback skills if you did an honest self-assessment?

Do you give frequent feedback to your colleagues?

Are you comfortable giving positive feedback?

What about negative (constructive) feedback?

Do you let people know right away what didn't work, was ineffective, or that they could do better?

Feedback is essential to learning, improvement, and team performance, yet many managers procrastinate or even avoid giving it. Why is this?

In our experience, it is human nature to want to avoid activities that we are not good at, or that make us feel uncomfortable. For all of the above reasons, feedback is an essential skill that managers must become proficient at. Managers who are committed to high performance on their teams and in their department must create a "feedback rich environment". Giving feedback is a little bit like learning a new sport. Take skiing, for example. Or tennis. Or golf. Almost everyone is poor at first until they get some formal training. Like these sports, giving feedback is just not something that comes naturally for most people.

Perhaps you are like a lot of us and have spent years avoiding giving feedback and missed those opportunities to practice and improve. Well, it's not too late. If you put the following guidelines and tips into practice, your feedback ability will begin to improve immediately. We have found that offering managers and leaders a simple set of steps or a simple formula is a great way to get them to practice it the right way so they develop the right habits.

A Simple, Effective Feedback Formula

There are numerous books, courses and guidance on ways to give feedback. We use a simple, yet effective feedback framework developed at the *Center for Creative Leadership* calls "S-B-I".

1. Situation

Describe the situation and provide the context in terms of why this behavior or aspect of performance is important to you, the team, or the organization. State your purpose and context for the feedback. (This is also known as framing).

"Tom, I want to give you some feedback about the Drexell proposal you recently completed".

2. Behavior

Name a specific observable behavior you want to call attention to. This should be a statement of fact, not a perception (interpretation or judgment), and it should not use labels (does not characterize the person).

"I understand you worked evenings and weekends to meet the deadline".

3. Impact

Share what the specific impact of that behavior has been on you, on the team, or on the business from your perspective, using "I statements". "I want you to know how much I appreciate your effort to go above and beyond what was expected to create such an excellent result". "I feel confident Drexell will respond positively". Using "I" statements conveys your own experience (and feelings) rather than characterizing the other person. Also, by owning your own experience, you are stating your impression or perspective and are not stating a fact (which promotes defensiveness or argumentativeness).

"Jack, your efforts last week with the Smith Account repaired a customer relationship I thought we had lost for good". "Your decision to offer an extra site inspection as a 'make-good' clearly worked. I am proud of how you handled the situation."

"Christina, I wanted to acknowledge the way you spoke so calmly with that upset customer." "He wasn't able to see why I couldn't do what he asked until you explained it. I really felt supported."

Why You Should Never Use "Labels" in Your Feedback

We are not suggesting that you avoid labels because it may make the "snowflakes" or "social justice warriors" in your office uncomfortable.

Note that I just deliberately used two labels there, to illustrate this point. You may have noticed a certain gut reaction to my use of labels. This illustrates the point. We should never use labels to describe an actual person we work with; that would be bad form, indeed.

I will explain exactly what we mean by "labels" and why you must avoid them.

Using labels not only makes some people uncomfortable; it is also politically incorrect, and could even be illegal in some states. It is bad for business. The use of labels creates a whole host of problems for managers and their companies.

Harvard Professors Robert Kegan and Lisa Lahey did extensive research on this which was incorporated in their excellent book, "How the Way We Talk Can Change the Way We Work: Seven Languages for Transformation".

Following are some examples of "positive labels" in the context of feedback.

"Steve, you are a good communicator."

"John is a total rockstar at sales." "If we characterize people, even if we do so quite positively, we actually engage— however unintentionally— in the rather presumptuous activity of entitling ourselves to say who and how the other is." "We dress the other person in a suit of psychological clothes", Kegan and Lahey explained.

As much as they might appreciate the fancy quality of the cloth, they are likely to feel, 'Well, it doesn't exactly fit.'" Rather than characterizing the person with a label, just use an "I statement" and share how you feel about his/her behavior (not his/her character or personality).

Following are the same examples of positive feedback, minus the labels.

"Steve, I really appreciate how you use stories to illustrate your points. I find it very compelling and helps drive the point home for me."

"John, I appreciate how you always prepare thoroughly and answer client objections skillfully."

The Problem with Using Labels When Giving Constructive Criticism

If the label is negative (constructive criticism), very likely, it's going to trigger defensiveness, argumentativeness, resentment, or even anger.

If the purpose of giving constructive feedback (criticism) is to help the other person improve by internalizing the feedback and changing his/her behavior, then using a label is self-defeating.

People tend to reject negative labels and close down on feedback.

When you use labels in your constructive feedback, the other person doesn't learn anything beyond the fact that you're suck at giving feedback.

Instead of this:

"Karen, you are showing up as unprofessional."

or

"You are sloppy."

Say this instead...

"Karen, I've noticed that you often have stacks of miscellaneous things on and under your desk." "I'm concerned that your workspace could reflect negatively on our department when a customer visits."

The Problem with Using Labels When Giving Positive Feedback

If the label is positive, the person receiving the feedback may not identify with that label (character trait), may feel uncomfortable or embarrassed by the positive label, and is likely to reject the compliment. "John is a rockstar salesman."

"John, you are a world class public speaker."

John may not feel comfortable being labeled a "rockstar" or a "world-class public speaker". That may not fit his self-concept. Or it may make him feel uncomfortable and want to reject the feedback (Aw, shucks, I just got lucky).

Here is how it would sound minus the label...

"John, I was so proud of the way that you overcame the client's objections using compelling case study data."

"John, when I know you are on the presentation team, I feel relaxed and confident because you are always prepared to answer client objections so skillfully." It is difficult for John to refute the factual statement of what happened or your feelings about how his behavior impacted you. Because he doesn't reject the positive feedback, he hears it and he is more likely to internalize it.

The Problem with Praise (and Why You Should Absolutely Stop Doing It)

"But what if the person being labeled with a positive trait actually likes and internalizes that positive label?", you may ask.. That's bad too. Actually, that's even worse. Not only does it not help the person, it may actually harm him/her .

Using positive labels (character traits) to describe people is precisely the thing that triggers what Stanford Professor Carol Dweck causes a "Fixed Mindset". Her research—which you can read about in her bestselling book, *Mindset: The New Psychology of Success*— shows that using positive labels can lead to a whole host of learning and performance issues both in children and especially in adults.

Note that we often refer to Dweck's "Fixed Mindset" as the "Knower" mindset (which you may recall from an earlier section entitled "Attitudes Toward Learning."

These issues include:

1. Becoming a "know it all"

2. Being afraid of making mistakes or feeling like a failure

3. Avoiding taking risks

4. Rejecting feedback and opportunities to improve

5. Fudging work or downright cheating (in a desperate attempt to live up to the internalized label)

Kegan and Lahey describe the positive feedback seen in most organizations as "praise and prizes".

Although this approach is intended to make people feel good, their research shows that it creates a cultural sense of "winners" and "losers" in the organization and diminishes, rather than increases, energy and morale.

Pro Tips for Giving Feedback

Be Specific and Concrete

Address the person directly and specify the context and behavior. Avoid generalizations such as "great," "poor," "inappropriate," or "outstanding".

The goal is for the person to understand what he should keep doing, start doing, or stop doing.

Timely

If you wait too long to give a colleague feedback, it won't be very useful. The best time to give feedback about a specific event, behavior, or performance is immediately following or as soon as possible (same day or next day).

Frequent

Leaders of high-performance teams cultivate a "feedback-rich environment". People should always know how they are doing, the quality of work they are delivering, and how they are "showing up" (being perceived by others). All workers are entitled to feedback about their job performance. Having said that, you must use your own judgment about how often you can offer feedback without making the person feel overwhelmed or saturated.

Focus on the Future More Than the Past

Rather than fixating on what the person did in the past, effective feedback emphasizes what will work better in the future. This is easily accomplished with phrases such as, "What might work better next time…" or "You might consider trying ____ the next time…."

Pro Tips for Giving Constructive Feedback

An executive in a leadership training program we conducted once referred to constructive feedback as an "uncomfortable conversation". In my experience, it's only uncomfortable if you aren't any good at it.

When you get good at giving feedback, it's a positive experience; it's an opportunity to help someone learn and an opportunity to support someone to have more success.

The keys to constructive, or critical, feedback are essentially the same as those for positive feedback, but the stakes are much higher.

Here are a few additional tips specific to giving constructive feedback.

Be Discreet

Always give constructive feedback in private, never in front of others. People may need to save face in front of their peers and digest what you have to say. Consider Feelings

Reflect ahead of time on the potential emotional impact of the feedback. How might the other person feel about it? You are probably familiar with the "sandwich" method.

You make a positive statement (bread), then give constructive feedback about what they can improve (the meat), and then a second positive statement in the form of reassurance or encouragement of some kind. This can be effective if you incorporate the other tips in this section and if it doesn't come across as formulaic or cheesy.

Can you think of some ways you can use the guidelines and tips in this section to get better at giving feedback? Is there a way to frame the next piece of feedback you give in a way that the other person is more likely to hear and benefit from it? Can you offer some kind of connection or reassurance that you care and are available for additional support if they need it? We'll end this section by offering you some feedback.

We believe that the very fact that you are studying this material tells us that you are genuinely interested in improving how you give feedback. And we feel confident that if you practice, you will get better, and that will make you a better manager and leader.

One of the "modes of communication" I introduced previously bears special emphasis. Leaders must be good listeners to be able to understand context (also called sensemaking), connect with employees (and colleagues), and influence individuals and teams. Poor listeners are never good leaders. Most leaders I have worked with (with a few exceptions) had room to elevate their listening skills.

Active Listening

Active listening is a powerfully effective tool that conscious communicators use to reveal the deeper meaning of communication.

Communication carries both fact and effect (feeling). Listening, as it is conventionally practiced, tends to focus on words and omits subtle and emotional subtext.

Active listening does not replace casual conversation or other modes of communication. Rather, it is a specific practice used when it is necessary to accurately understand someone's perspective.

There are two aspects to the practice of active listening:

1. Adopting an "active listening mindset";

2. Learning and utilizing specific active listening techniques, which, with practice, mature into listening skills.

The Active Listening Mindset

Active listening requires a specific mindset grounded in a "seek to understand" orientation. Intentionally shifting into this mindset helps open up conversation space for more meaningful communication.

Active listening is about deeply connecting with the other person, being genuinely interested in their experience and perspective, and really hearing what they are saying.

People can tell when you're not being sincere. Authenticity is how people decide if they can trust you. It's hard to pretend to be authentic, so try to avoid situations where you can't be genuine when listening. If you're short on time or have an agenda for the conversation, wait until you have more time to practice active listening. It takes some skill and effort to really listen actively. If you can do it, you're well on your way.

The listening techniques and skills described in the following section are complementary to this mindset. But if you aren't in an active listening mindset in the first place, the following techniques aren't very helpful.

Listen Without Deciding

The first step in active listening is to set your agenda aside while you seek to deeply understand the other person's point of view.

So, it follows that when adopting an active listening mindset, your intention is to understand, not to decide. Evaluation and decision-making may come after the active listening session. Considering other people's perspectives does not require or even involve abandoning your own perspective. On the contrary, other vantage points often serve to enrich your own understanding of a topic. Listening without deciding refers to an inherently nonjudgmental approach to listening.

Rather than trying to anticipate what the speaker will say or becoming preoccupied with right or wrong, be curious about his/her experience, assumptions, and conclusions.

Give Undivided Attention

Presence is useful for everyone, but for leaders, it is especially important. One of the easiest and best ways leaders can show up as present is through the practice of active listening.

Being present means paying attention to the speaker and really focusing on what they're saying. Think about a time when you talked to someone who was really present - they listened to you and made you feel heard. On the other hand, we've all talked to someone who wasn't present - they seemed distracted or not fully there. Everyone notices when someone is or isn't present. Active listening means focusing on the other person and making sure they feel heard and understood. This means taking the time and space to be present. If you find your mind wandering or thinking about what to say next, active listening can help you bring your attention back.

Maintain Eye Contact

When you're actively listening, make sure to use eye contact, good posture, and good breathing. With practice, you can use your body to stay present in the conversation. Your body can show your true feelings without you even realizing it. So, it's important to keep eye contact and a relaxed, engaged posture. A relaxed posture shows you're receptive.

Avoid Listening Autobiographically

When Listening, it's natural to relate to what's being said and feel empathy. But when you start talking about your own experiences and stories, it takes the focus off the person speaking and makes it about you. In the context of active listening, this is kind of like taking over the conversation. While it's okay to share your own experiences in a conversation, it's not active listening. To practice active listening, keep the focus on the other person and save your stories for later. There will be time for discussion or advocacy after actively listening.

Active Listening Skills

Once you can shift into an active listening mindset, the following active listening skills can really take your active listening practice to the next level.

Some programs teach these as "techniques" or "tactics". We prefer to think of them as skills. The practice of active listening involves five specific skills.

Questioning

Questioning demonstrates your intent to understand, invites the speaker to elaborate, and helps to tease out key ideas for greater clarity.

Avoid "yes" or "no" questions. By asking open-ended questions, the speaker has an opportunity to reveal what she deems relevant and important.

Rather than say, "Did you think the meeting went well?" ask, "What was your impression of the meeting?"

Examples:

"What's your opinion on this?"

"Tell me about..."

"What happened next?"

Ask an open-ended question about something you want to talk about. The person will probably bring up a few topics. Ask follow-up questions about those topics, which we call "doors". It's like giving you permission to ask more about that topic since they brought it up. For instance, if they mention their family or a problem they're having, you can ask more about it because they brought it up. You pick which "doors" to go through by asking about the most interesting topics. You may have started the conversation with a specific question, but once it starts, you can steer it by choosing which doors to go through.

Reflecting

Reflecting involves paraphrasing or restating what you have heard so far. This lets the speaker know that you are following the conversation and understanding the key points.

It also demonstrates your intention to understand. This usually encourages the speaker to open up a little more.

Examples:

"What I'm hearing you say is..."

"If I understand you correctly..."

Empathizing

Empathizing is the practice of tuning in emotionally to how the other person is feeling. While empathizing is certainly an important leadership communication "skill," it is also an emotional intelligence competency.

Like all emotional and social intelligence competencies, some people are naturally better at it than others.

In his bestselling book, *Working with Emotional Intelligence*, Daniel Goleman describes empathy as our "social radar".

Empathy is when you can sense how someone else feels without them telling you. It's about picking up on their tone of voice, facial expressions, and other nonverbal cues. It's about understanding how they feel without adding your own thoughts or feelings. If you can, try to relate to their emotions by thinking back to a time when you felt something similar. But don't just share your own feelings - that's called listening "autobiographically". Studies show that leaders with high empathy skills tend to do better than those who aren't tuned into others' emotions.

Examples:

"I sense your disappointment about..."

"It seems like that situation was very frustrating for you."

Clarifying

To clarify, ask follow-up questions about who, what, when, why, and how, and give the speaker an opportunity to bring more nuance to their sharing.

This is your opportunity to confirm an accurate understanding of what is being expressed. This is your opportunity to gauge the "intent" versus the "impact".

If there is a perceived gap between intent and impact, the speaker can be guided to restate, reframe, or further elaborate so you can understand what she actually intended.

Clarifying is absolutely critical when you are engaged in a high-stakes conversation or one with a complex story line that could easily be confused or misunderstood.

Examples:

"That last part was a bit unclear to me. Can you say more?"

"Can you give me an example to illustrate what you mean?"

Summarizing

Before the conversation turns to a new topic, it's a good idea to pause and offer a summary of the speaker's key themes.

It is useful to break the conversation down into two or three main sections (like acts in a play), each having a few main points that can be articulated concisely.

This helps the speaker feel a sense of closure for that portion of the conversation and allows him to move on to the next.

Summarizing at the very end of the conversation is even more important.

Summarizing ensures that the speaker feels heard and that you can both move to closure.

Ending abruptly can feel quite jarring and diminish the positive connection the active listening created. When wrapping up, ask a question like, "Is there anything else?"

Examples:

"The key theme of what you're sharing with me seems to be..."

"What I'm taking away from what you said is..."

Practicing active listening takes time, but the more you do it, the better you'll get. Anytime someone talks to you at work or home, you can use that as an opportunity to practice. Just remember, everything in moderation, including active listening. It's not always the right mode of communication and you can't do it all the time. It's about giving undivided attention, empathy, and connecting with someone, but that's not always possible.

Do not attempt active listening in situations when:

1) You don't have the time to allow the conversation to unfold for at least 5–15 minutes (and maybe more).

2) You don't have the mental bandwidth to set aside distractions and give the other person undivided attention.

3) You don't have the emotional presence or spaciousness to empathize with the other person and connect with their feelings and your own.

Active listening is a powerful tool. Use it often but use it deliberately when the situation warrants it.

This important leadership communication skill will have an additive effect on many of the other leadership techniques and skills you're learning in this book.

Dialogue and Collaboration

This section is designed to be a primer for the work mode referred to as "collaboration" and the specific communication mode called "dialogue." For some leaders, collaboration and dialogue come naturally and intuitively. Others find these to be less intuitive and even a bit awkward.

For reasons that will become even more clear in this lesson, it is essential that you, in your role as manager, dial in your ability to collaborate on projects and assignments skillfully.

The specific skill of dialogue enables you to move your projects successfully across the finish line each month and each quarter. And these skills expand your versatility as a manager and leader.

We will start with collaboration and then offer a few tips for better dialogue. The dictionary definition of collaboration is "the action of working with someone to produce or create something."

If you recall the section entitled "Modes of Communication" then you are very familiar with collaboration and why it is so important.

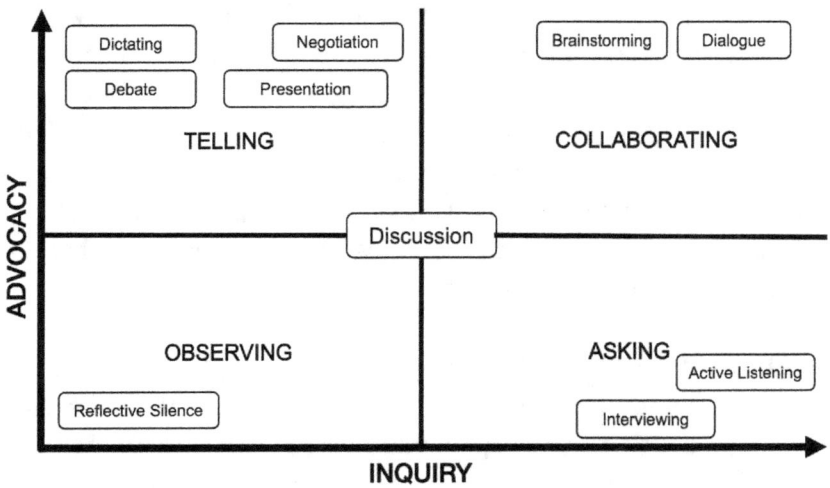

The Modes of Communication framework posits two dimensions of communication: telling and asking. Communication experts sometimes use the terms "advocacy" for telling and "inquiry" for asking.

As mentioned earlier in this chapter, most managers are trained to be "advocates"—to assert a point of view, debate, and influence—in an attempt to solve problems and achieve goals. But as they move into senior positions and confront more complex and diverse issues, advocacy that is not balanced with inquiry becomes problematic. High advocacy can polarize communication with limited possible outcomes: Either person A may win, or person B may win, or both may walk away with their views unchanged (and may not feel very good about the interaction).

Most people communicate habitually—completely unaware of the broad range of choices available to them. In fact, most people use only one or two modes of communication (e.g., discussion and debate) and do not take advantage of the full range of communication modes available. Different circumstances call for different approaches to communication. People with greater awareness of a situation and a variety of modes to choose from bring greater versatility to communication and can achieve significantly better outcomes.

Clearly, as a manager and leader, you must develop versatility with both of these. As you progress in your career as a manager and your skills as a leader, you will expand your repertoire so that you can easily draw upon multiple modes of communication that are called for in different situations.

Clearly, as a manager and leader, you are required to draw on many modes of communication. Some circumstances call for giving presentations or being very direct and telling employees what they need to do (high advocacy). In some cases, you observe, and in others, you interview job candidates which involves mostly asking questions and listening (high inquiry).

When you run effective meetings, you will need to draw on several of these modes including: presenting, delegating, brainstorming, active listening, and of course, dialogue. When you engage your strategic thinking skills, especially in group environments, and when you conduct your strategic planning, especially when you are prioritizing opportunities and projects (all topics of other lessons) you will have to draw on all of the above modes plus perhaps some reflective silence and even some debating and negotiation. Similarly, in order to implement your project management and feedback skills (also covered in other lessons), you must demonstrate a certain level of communication versatility as you switch back and forth between advocacy and inquiry modes.

Why is Collaboration So Important in Today's Work Environment

There are several reasons why collaboration has become increasingly important in today's fast-paced, diverse global business environments.

Faster-paced industries with rapid innovation require many perspectives to stay informed and stay competitive.

As access to knowledge proliferates via the internet at an even faster pace, we must consult multiple experts with different experiences to understand complex situations.

Younger generations raised in diverse, global "post-modern" cultures expect to be heard, to have their perspectives respected, and to have input into the work efforts they are a part of. In short, many expect collaborative work places.

Research on high-performance organizations that are adaptive, innovate quickly, and thrive in fast-paced market conditions shows that collaboration is a prerequisite to stay competitive.

Fast-emerging communication platforms that allow people to work remotely (via phone and video conferencing) and asynchronously (email, project management platforms, and messaging platforms) demand that managers have good collaboration skills just to keep up.

These are just a few of the reasons. Perhaps you can think of more.

Tactics and Practices that Leaders Can Use to Encourage Collaboration

Let's explore some best practices that, as a manager and leader, you can encourage your team and co-workers to experiment with and adopt.

Cultivating a Collaboration Mindset

It is helpful to remember and remind your peers that when teams collaborate effectively, they produce new ideas and innovative solutions that can help everyone have more success with less stress as they work together toward shared goals.

You do not need to think the same, share the same ideas or be close friends to collaborate. Collaboration is based on mutual respect and an appreciation that two heads (and sets of hands) are better than one. Bringing an appreciation for the other person's worldview, perspective, experience, and diverse skills is a great foundation for your collaboration mindset.

In a later section of this book, we will explore *"Working With Assumptions and Interpretations."* This is extremely important for collaboration. When cultivating a collaboration mindset, it is essential to give the other people the benefit of the doubt and assume they know what they are talking about and are able to bring professionalism to the collaboration.

For many, it is too easy to quickly jump to conclusions and assume wrongly that they don't understand something or aren't competent.

It is crucial to guard against this tendency to allow for the most productive collaborations. And, managers are wise to avoid leaving bad impressions with people who they may depend upon to secure future successes.

Cultivating a Collaborative Work Environment

Building on the collaboration mindset we just discussed, it is also important that you cultivate a collaborative environment. Perhaps it is easier to understand this by considering work environments that inhibit, block or obstruct collaboration.

Things such as….

Silos in which different departments rarely communicate with one-another.

Toxic environments in which people feel the need to be protective or keep their heads down to avoid criticism, turf wars, or retaliations of some kind.

Overly rigid and regimented environments that encourage conformity and discourage self-expression, creativity, or "outside the box" thinking.

Physical work environments in which people are separated and have little opportunity to engage in "water cooler conversations."

Perhaps you can think of other environmental factors that discourage collaboration.

Some of the environments that can promote collaboration, include: Cross-functional teams where people with different disciplines have opportunities to meet each other, exchange ideas and share challenges.

Leadership styles and cultures value differences and uniqueness where people are encouraged to be self-expressive while more openly sharing their ideas.

Meeting rhythms that give people an opportunity to "get out of their usual lane" and participate in conversations about new topics with new people whom they may not interact with on a daily basis..

An environment that values conversation and encourages people to get to know one another, cultivate shared interests, and make the time to help each other on projects.

Cultivating Psychological Safety

If we overlay the "leadership paradigms" we can easily see that the "Imperial" and "Traditional" paradigms, that rely on fear and intimidation (and authority) do not value "psychological safety" very much. The "Modern" leadership paradigm sees the value in it but it is not a primary concern (especially if employees and teams are performing). This brings us to the "Postmodern" paradigm. As you no doubt can appreciate, this paradigm elevates "psychological safety" up to the highest level of priority along with "diversity, equity and inclusion." So, if you have leaders who subscribe to this paradigm, this will be very important. Also, if you have followers who have the "Affiliative" mindset (a.k.a. the Postmodern worldview) then you better make damn sure you put a lot of emphasis on psychological safety because that is what they expect from "legitimate leaders" (in their view) who use the "Humanistic" leadership style. Clearly, Humanistic leaders cultivate psychological safety.

Why has the topic of psychological safety become so common today. Well, it is important in general, but it is especially important with organizations that are influenced by the "Postmodern" leadership paradigm (or have leaders or consultants) influencing the organization that have an Affiliative mindset (Postmodern worldview).

A substantial body of research has been done and much has been written about psychological safety. We now know that this is a key factor in employee engagement, job satisfaction, effective teamwork, and yes, collaboration (especially with workers and teams with the Affiliative mindset).

Team members benefit from being able to come together and expect that people will treat one another with respect. If people don't feel safe sharing their ideas, speaking up, and taking some social risks, then collaboration will be stunted.

The key to creating a sense of psychological safety in your teams boils down to empathy and kindness. As a manager and leader, you can model empathy for your teams.

Try to deeply understand your peers, including how they work, where their expertise lies, the challenges they deal with, especially by empathizing with how they feel about all these things.

Naturally, it is important to show respect and kindness at every opportunity. The more you cultivate these qualities in your culture, the better the collaboration will be.

Making Space in Your Meetings for Collaboration

Effective Meetings is a topic of another lesson in this course. Clearly, to promote collaboration you have to make space on the agenda for it during key meetings.

This requires some spaciousness. It also requires some silent observation, more inquiry than advocacy, to draw people out, especially teammates that appear to be more introverted.

Encourage your team members to get to know each other, in particular, to understand one another's individual responsibilities and projects.

It goes without saying that when groups of people come together who have good dialogue skills, the collaboration will be enhanced.

Dialogue

As you will recall, the mode of communication that we call dialogue is situated in the far upper-right portion of our Modes of Communication diagram.

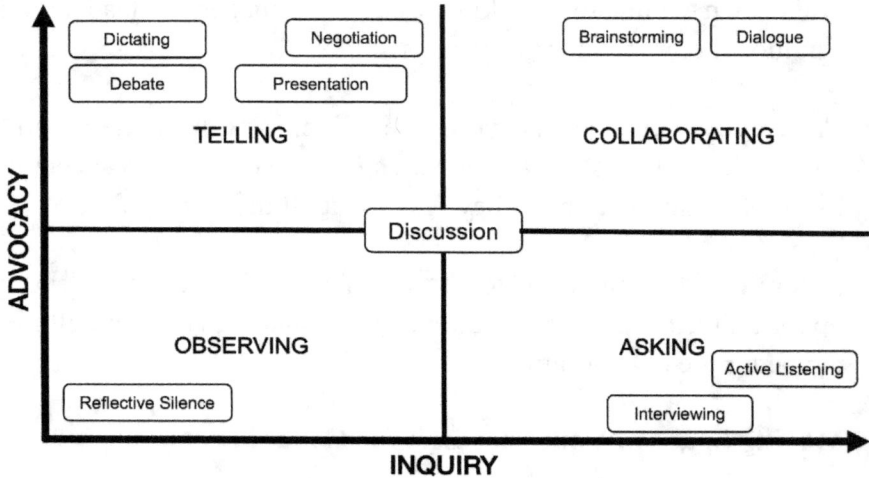

This mode (high advocacy, high inquiry) seeks to get all relevant views out into the open in order to facilitate a shared understanding of the issues at hand.

As noted earlier, dialogue is especially useful in situations where complex and/or difficult business issues need to be considered from multiple vantage points.

Dialogue actually reflects a collaborative mindset and cultivates a collaborative environment!

The word "dialogue" is derived from the Greek term *dialegesthai*, also known as "dialectical communication."

Contrasted with debate, negotiation or presentation, when people dialogue, the goal is to come to a new understanding.

Dialogue implies a reciprocal, mutually-enriching communication interaction. It requires the ability to fluidly shift back and forth between inquiry (asking) and advocacy (telling) to be successful.

The main difference between discussion and dialogue is that in the latter, parties willingly set their agendas aside, suspend their interpretations and judgments, and engage in active listening for the purpose of uncovering deeper issues that might otherwise not surface using other modes of communication.

When dialogue is successful, both parties feel heard and understood as a result of the interaction. And, perhaps most importantly, the dialogue has yielded new insights and valuable pathways forward that neither party possessed beforehand.

Dialogue requires trust. When we dialogue, we generously share both our ideas and our feelings. And we have to be genuinely interested in the other person's perspectives.

One of the best ways to enhance the skill of dialogue is to practice active listening.

When you dialogue, you spend some time sharing (advocating) your feelings and perspectives. But when it is time to listen, it is best to engage in active listening. In this way, your dialogue partner is most likely to feel heard, and empathized with.

Again, when you can fluidly shift between advocacy and inquiry as we have been exploring, the people you manage and work with will develop greater trust in you and become more willing to share.

Another excellent pathway to improve your dialogue skills is to observe people who are good at it.

When you do, you will notice that they seem genuinely interested in other perspectives, they allow space for the other person's experience, views, and expertise.

People who are good at dialogue can often be seen "leaning in" and welcoming differences with curiosity and interpersonal warmth. Rather than treating the communication as a debate or competition of some kind, they try to weave the perspectives together into a richer tapestry of shared understanding.

As you cultivate more collaboration in your workplace, and especially as you practice and strengthen your dialogue skills, you will significantly boost your ability to add value to your organization as a manager and leader.

The next skill is absolutely essential for effective leadership. Yet, this is a skill that is not often taught to managers and executives. You will never go beyond intermediate in your leadership skill until you get really good at "working with assumptions and interpretations." So please make sure to adopt this practice and teach it to every one of the employees who report to you. It is absolutely critical.

Working With Assumptions and Interpretations

Have you ever left a meeting and thought to yourself, "What world is he living in? "I don't understand why he thinks that."

This phrase—or some version of it—is heard often among your peers, your employees, and yes, your boss. How often have you come into a meeting with a colleague (or client) with seemingly the same information about some sticky situation, but they have drawn totally different conclusions than you?

What do you do in those situations?

You don't necessarily want to be in a position to have to tell them they are wrong, educate them, or give some kind of play-by-play so they understand what is actually happening.

One of the main difficulties in human relations, and leadership in particular, is that people interpret the same set of facts very differently. We all have experienced conversations with a client or colleague and wondered, "How on earth have they concluded that from these facts"? But these are only the moments we actually catch.

It's a little bit overwhelming to think how many times we've made statements we haven't fully thought through. And another person makes an assumption about our motives, and capabilities, or draws conclusions we would prefer they hadn't.

Organizational life has a lot of challenges, abundant with assumptions, misunderstandings, and even what we call "drama".

The problem is that many (perhaps even most) people don't communicate their assumptions and interpretations as such. They tend to state their thinking as if that is the reality.

Worse, many people actually believe that their thinking about reality is the actual reality. Of course, this creates a lot of problems for managers.

Well, if that's the bad news, the good news is that there is a simple framework you can learn and keep in mind in your role as a manager.

This skill can help you avoid 80% of the conflicts that are actually avoidable, that is caused by misunderstandings that resulted from the mishandling of assumptions and wrong interpretations.

"Making meaning" is fundamental to the practice of management and leadership. If you want your ideas to positively influence others, then you need to understand and be understood. Clearly, meaning is a function of how people interpret things.

What a given set of facts "mean" is going to be different from person to person.

People tend to think their perceptions of reality (including their interpretations) are objective facts. Your peers, reports and even your boss often treat their interpretations as facts. Without even considering that other people have equally valid (and perhaps even more accurate) interpretations of those very same facts.

If you are serious about being successful in your role as manager, you need to understand others and communicate with them in a way that you are understood (at least most of the time).

The Ladder of Inference

In this book we will use a simple metaphor to help leaders work more skillfully with this process of interpretation. The "Ladder of Inference" is a framework that was conceived by Harvard's Chris Argyris and later popularized by MIT's Peter Senge and proponents of the field of organizational learning. If you can use this framework to make sure that both you and the person you are speaking with have your ladders "leaning against the same wall", then you can eliminate a lot of headaches and create a much more positive impact in the work you do.

The "Ladder of Inference" is a step-by-step process, like climbing the rungs of a ladder, that provides a really useful framework that helps us see, at a glance, how the process unfolds—often in a split second—that leads to our conclusions (our inferences). This "ladder" has five rungs on it.

1. We observe an event

In doing so, we experience sights, sounds, and feelings.

2. We select partial data

We look for, notice, and select certain data to emphasize while (often unconsciously) ignoring other data.

3. We filter that data through our worldview

Our worldview includes our values and general beliefs (about people and the world), as well as specific beliefs about the type of situation currently being perceived. It is our worldview that initially transforms objective data (facts) into subjective meaning (interpretation).

4. We make assumptions

We rarely (if ever) have all the relevant information and perspectives at our disposal in a given situation. There are always details and nuances that are invisible to us, including facts we lack about what happened (or is happening), the intention or motivation of people involved, and the consequences (often yet to be seen) of certain specific actions.

Because people aren't omniscient, and time rarely permits obtaining and verifying every piece of relevant information, we draw conclusions through a subjective assessment of which facts are most relevant based on generalizations (general principles or broad patterns of behavior).

5. Finally, we draw conclusions

Based on our climb up the ladder, we form an inference, a conclusion. These conclusions, in turn, inform the actions we take. Our conclusions not only shape our beliefs about a person or situation but also impact the data that we seek, perceive, and emphasize when encountering similar circumstances in the future

In this way the ladder of inference is self-reinforcing. Put another way, we interpret situations through our worldview which reinforces our subjective perception of the world (our worldview).

With each step up the ladder, there is an opportunity for different people's stories to diverge. Interpersonal communication and relationships become difficult when people stay on the highest rung of the ladder (their conclusions) without stepping down to where most of the real action is.... the way we interpret the data to arrive at different conclusions.

The key to unlocking interpersonal communication, relationships, motivation, and influence is to focus not on the conclusions, but on the way that people interpret (and misinterpret) information. Here are some questions to reflect on that will help you avoid and minimize conflict caused by assumptions and interpretations.

Have the facts that they are focusing on been made explicit?

What assumptions might others be making about the people and the circumstances involved?

(And the same goes for you.) Can you climb the ladder consciously rather than unconsciously?

Are you explicitly communicating the facts you are aware of to the people you are speaking to?

What assumptions are you making about the people and the circumstances involved?

Are you framing those as assumptions, or stating those assumptions as objective facts? This tends to put others on the defensive.

By applying this framework in your work as a manager, first, your own interpretations tend to be more accurate.

Second, the previously obscured process by which others interpret situations, information and communication becomes far more transparent. In this way, you are better at understanding and at being understood as a manager.

Here again, I am about to introduce a leadership communication skill that separates ineffective leaders from effective leaders. The best leaders you know do this very well despite the fact that this skill is not taught in many trainings. If you are to have long-term success as a leader, especially if you want to move beyond intermediate skill level to advanced, then you absolutely need to master the art of "framing."

Framing

In a previous section entitled *Intent vs. Impact,* I suggested that one of the best ways to adjust your message to accommodate the listener's mindset is the practice of framing.

To understand this crucial communication skill, it's useful to revisit our iceberg metaphor and the concepts of "pretext" and "subtext."

The explicit message—the words and the "face value" of what is being said —is the pretext. The listener is not aware of all the information the speaker has, including any number of assumptions being made. The deeper meaning of the communication is often submerged as subtext.

It has been said that all meaning is context dependent. This is true. The subtext—or context of the communication—can be thought of as the bulk of the iceberg that lies beneath the surface. It is implicitly present, but often, people fail to make it explicit.

This may seem like a subtle nuance, but it's more than that. It is one of the main causes of unnecessary and avoidable misunderstandings and relationship- and career-damaging interpersonal conflict.

When you fail to make the subtext explicit, listeners often fail to understand the purpose of the conversation, misinterpret your intentions, or misunderstand the meaning of the message.

Conscious communicators deliberately make the subtext explicit, state the reason and purpose for the discussion, make their assumptions explicit, and let the listener know why the topic is relevant to them. Subtext can also be referred to as the "frame of reference," or "frame," for short.

According to integral communication theorist and former Boston College professor Bill Torbert, framing is the element of communication most often missing from conversations and meetings. He explains, "The speaker too often assumes the other knows and shares the overall objective ... Explicit framing is useful precisely because the assumption of a shared frame is frequently untrue."

When speakers merely assume a shared understanding of the subtext and fail to frame the communication, listeners need to guess about their agenda and what point they are driving toward. When forced to guess at a frame, people frequently guess wrong.

Too often, the guessing takes a negative slant. For example, "Why is he bringing this up now? He must not trust me." Or, "What is he getting at? Is he implying that I did something wrong?" Without a clear frame, it is easy to assume others have negative or manipulative motives.

Many people's frames are unconscious, especially the fundamental assumptions inherent in their worldview (i.e., their values, beliefs, assumptions, and motivations).

Recognizing Other People's Frames

Have you ever been in the middle of a conversation and thought, "He thinks I agree with him. I don't even agree with his basic assumption—but he seems to think that I do!"

When we communicate unconsciously without being aware of, clarifying, and/or fully understanding the other person's frame, we can inadvertently accept their frame or at least give the other person that impression. If you don't pause and clarify the context (background and assumptions), then you are, by default, accepting their assumptions and interpretations about the situation.

Take the time to present the context. Ask clarifying questions about the background of the situation, what they know, and what assumptions they are making. "John, can we back up for a minute and make sure I'm on the same page with you in terms of the purpose of this conversation? I assume we are here to decide on an action plan for closing the California plant and that you are concerned about severance packages. Is that right?"

How To Use Framing When Delivering Messages

When communicating, it is crucial that you make the context explicit using framing. In this way, you can check to see if the listener shares your frame (i.e., has the same information and accepts the assumptions you are making about it). By framing, you let the listener know why this message is important and why they should care. Framing promotes clarity, prevents confusion, and most importantly, aligns intent with impact.

You can use framing to address relevancy, state purpose and intentions, expose assumptions, and check for agreement. With practice, you can learn to recognize other people's mindsets (i.e., their assumptions, attitudes, worldview, and motivation) and frame your communication so it is more resonant with their mindset and more understandable to them. You may find that you use framing more than any other communication skill introduced in this module.

Foundational Framing

As your framing skills grow, the first level of framing is what I call "Foundational Framing." Foundational framing is simply framing in terms of the five foundations: relevancy, intentions, checking for agreement, and motivation.

Address Relevancy

"Our ability to stay on budget with this project will directly affect our performance bonus. That's why we need to keep close tabs on the numbers."

State Your Purpose and Intentions

"I want to hear about what happened in the client meeting yesterday so I can be prepared for my presentation next week."

Make Your Assumptions Explicit

"I assume you are familiar with the cost optimization initiative. If that's true, I'd like to get your feedback on how you think the project is going."

Check for Agreement on Purpose and Assumptions

"As I understand it, we are meeting to discuss some concerns that have been expressed about Sally's performance. Is that your understanding, as well?"

Make your communication motivating by connecting to the listener's mindset

"I know you are really competitive and love to win! So, I thought you
would really appreciate this opportunity to take your performance to the next level."

Once you have some practice with "Foundational Framing," now you are ready to continue to expand your framing skills with the next level of framing nuance which is what I call "Precision Framing."

Precision Framing

I call the next level "Precision Framing." There are 20 types of frames that I include in my "Top 20" precision framing methods. Below I will explain each and give you a real life example. When you combine the five "Fundamental Frames" above with the below 20 "Precision Frames" that then you will have a robust tool kit of 25 highly-specific frames that can be used to help make your message more influential and motivating.

Gain-Loss Framing

Gain-Loss framing involves focusing on the potential benefits (gains) or drawbacks (losses) of a decision or action. Leaders can use this frame to highlight the positive outcomes of adopting a new initiative or the negative consequences of maintaining the status quo.

Example:

Context: During a project team meeting, a leader is discussing an upcoming marketing initiative with a project manager. The discussion revolves around whether to invest in an ambitious new marketing strategy.

"If we embrace this new strategy, we stand to gain significant market exposure and attract new customers (gain frame). However, if we don't proceed with this, we risk losing ground to our competitors (loss frame)."

Attribution Framing

Attribution framing involves attributing the cause of events to either internal or external factors. Leaders can use this frame to acknowledge the team's efforts (internal attribution) or to highlight factors beyond their control (external attribution).

Example:

Context: In a one-on-one performance review, a leader is discussing an employee's recent sales performance. The conversation is about a decline in sales performance.

"Your sales figures have dipped this quarter, which seems largely due to the new competitor in our region (external attribution). However, I've noticed you've been proactive in seeking additional training to improve your skills (internal attribution)."

Issue Framing

Issue framing refers to how leaders present and define an issue, problem, or decision. By strategically framing an issue, leaders can influence how their team perceives the situation and, consequently, how they respond to it.

Context: During a senior executive meeting, a CEO is discussing potential layoffs. The issue is whether to proceed with layoffs due to financial difficulties.

"We could look at this situation purely in terms of financial sustainability, or we could consider it as an opportunity to streamline our operations and focus on our core strengths."

Relation Framing

Relation framing is about presenting the relationship between different entities or concepts. Leaders can use this frame to highlight teamwork, collaboration, competition, or hierarchy, depending on what's most relevant to the situation.

Example:

Context: A team leader is addressing their team about a new cross-functional project during a team meeting. The team leader needs to explain the relationship between their team and another department involved in the project.

"Our partnership with the IT department is not about who does more work. It's about collaboration, bringing our individual strengths to achieve a common goal."

Identity Framing

Identity framing involves linking decisions or actions to the team or organization's identity. By reminding the team of who they are and what they stand for, leaders can inspire action that aligns with the group's values and goals.

Example:

Context: During a town-hall meeting, a CEO is discussing the company's new strategic direction with all employees. The CEO needs to explain why the company is moving towards a more digital business model.

"As pioneers in our industry, we've always been at the forefront of change. This digital transformation reflects who we are—innovative, adaptable, and forward-thinking."

Temporal Framing

Temporal framing refers to how leaders use time to frame a situation or decision. They might focus on lessons from the past, actions in the present, or goals for the future, depending on what best serves their purpose.

Example:

Context: A project manager is addressing their team about project delays during a project update meeting. The project manager needs to discuss how to get back on track with the project timeline.

"Let's learn from our past challenges (past frame), focus on what we can do right now to accelerate progress (present frame), and keep our eyes on the ultimate project delivery date (future frame)."

Possibility vs. Necessity Framing

This frame juxtaposes the potential opportunities of a decision (possibility) against its essential requirement (necessity). Leaders can use this frame to highlight a choice's attractiveness or indispensability.

Example:

Context: A department head is discussing the adoption of a new software tool with an IT manager. They're discussing whether to move forward with the software implementation.

Example: "This new software presents us with the opportunity to drastically improve our efficiency (possibility frame). However, considering our recent scalability issues, adopting this new tool seems indispensable (necessity frame)."

Risk Framing

Risk framing involves discussing the potential risks associated with a decision or action. Leaders can use this frame to encourage caution, promote risk-taking, or balance risk against potential rewards.

Example:

Context: A leader is discussing a risky business proposition with a business development manager. The decision to be made is whether to enter a new, uncertain market.

Example: "Entering this new market certainly comes with risks, but if we plan carefully and leverage our unique strengths, it could open up significant growth opportunities."

Value Framing

Value framing involves linking decisions or actions to the values of the individual, team, or organization. By highlighting how a decision aligns with these values, leaders can inspire action that feels meaningful and purposeful.

Example:

Context: A team leader is discussing a new initiative with their team during a team meeting. The team leader is trying to motivate the team to participate in the new initiative.

Example: "Participating in this initiative not only helps us reach our quarterly targets, but it also aligns perfectly with our core value of continuous learning."

Proactive vs. Reactive Framing

This framing juxtaposes taking action before problems occur (proactive) versus responding after they've occurred (reactive). Leaders can use this frame to encourage foresight and preventative action or to validate responses to unexpected situations.

Example:

Context: A manager is discussing a change in market trends with a marketing executive. The manager needs to decide on adjusting their marketing strategy based on the new trends.

Example: "We can adjust our strategy now to anticipate these new trends (proactive frame), or we can wait until our sales are affected and then revise our approach (reactive frame)."

Emotional vs. Rational Framing

Emotional framing appeals to people's feelings, while rational framing appeals to logic and reason. Leaders can use these frames to engage their team's emotions, provide logical explanations, or balance emotion with reason.

Example:

Context: A team leader is discussing a difficult client with a customer service representative. The team leader needs to guide the representative on how to handle the client.

Example: "I understand dealing with this client can be frustrating (emotional frame). Let's look at the facts and determine the best strategy to meet their needs without compromising our standards (rational frame)."

Inclusive vs. Exclusive Framing

Inclusive framing involves all parties in the conversation, while exclusive framing singles out specific individuals or groups. Leaders can use these frames to foster a sense of collective identity or to acknowledge individual contributions.

Example:

Context: During a company-wide meeting, a CEO is discussing the impact of a recent merger. The CEO needs to address the concerns and questions employees have about the merger.

Example: "This merger is a step forward for all of us, and every department plays a crucial role in its success (inclusive frame). I want to especially acknowledge the finance team for their exceptional work during this transition (exclusive frame)."

Progress vs. Inertia Framing

Progress framing emphasizes moving forward and improving, while inertia framing focuses on the status quo or potential stagnation. Leaders can use these frames to inspire progress or caution against complacency.

Example:

Context: A sales manager is discussing quarterly performance with the sales team during a team meeting. The sales manager needs to address the team's performance and set goals for the next quarter.

Example: "We've made significant progress in expanding our client base this quarter (progress frame). If we don't capitalize on this momentum, we risk losing these potential opportunities (inertia frame)."

Hope vs. Fear Framing

Hope framing highlights positive future possibilities, while fear framing underscores potential negative outcomes. Leaders can use these frames to inspire optimism or caution, depending on the situation and desired response.

Example:

Context: A project manager is discussing a critical project delay with the project team during a team meeting. The project manager needs to motivate the team to work through the delay.

Example: "I'm confident that we can get back on track and deliver an excellent product (hope frame). However, if we don't address these issues now, our project's success might be in jeopardy (fear frame)."

Strategic vs. Tactical Framing

Strategic framing focuses on long-term goals and overarching strategies, while tactical framing zooms in on short-term objectives and specific actions. Leaders can use these frames to emphasize the big picture, the details, or the connection between the two.

Example:

Context: During a strategy meeting, a leader is discussing upcoming initiatives with department heads. The leader is outlining the company's strategic plan for the next fiscal year.

Example: "We need to focus on expanding our market share and enhancing our product portfolio (strategic frame). This will involve targeted marketing campaigns and focused product development efforts (tactical frame)."

Process vs. Outcome Framing

Process framing emphasizes how work is done, while outcome framing focuses on the results of that work. Leaders can use these frames to stress the importance of the journey, the destination, or both.

Example:

Context: A manager is discussing a project's progress with a project engineer. The discussion revolves around the project's progress and any adjustments needed.

Example: "It's important to follow our project roadmap and protocols (process frame), with the goal of delivering a high-quality end product on schedule (outcome frame)."

Challenge vs. Threat Framing

Challenge framing portrays a situation as an opportunity to learn and grow, while threat framing depicts it as a potential danger or loss. Leaders can use these frames to motivate their team to rise to a challenge or to caution against potential threats.

Example:

Context: During a crisis management meeting, a CEO is discussing a recent public relations crisis with the PR manager. The discussion revolves around handling the public relations crisis.

Example: "This crisis presents an opportunity for us to demonstrate our accountability and commitment to our customers (challenge frame). However, if we don't handle it correctly, our reputation might suffer significantly (threat frame)."

Personal vs. Professional Framing

Personal framing involves the personal aspects or interests of the team, while professional framing emphasizes the professional or work-related aspects. Leaders can use these frames to connect with their team on a personal level or to maintain a professional focus.

Example:

Context: In a one-on-one meeting, a leader is discussing career development with an employee. The leader is providing feedback and guidance for the employee's career progression.

"You've expressed a personal interest in leadership roles (personal frame), and there are upcoming managerial positions that align with your professional growth objectives (professional frame)."

Individual vs. Collective Framing

Individual framing focuses on the individual's role and responsibilities, while collective framing emphasizes the group's shared tasks and goals. Leaders can use these frames to acknowledge individual contributions or to foster a sense of collective identity and teamwork.

Example:

Context: A team leader is addressing their team about individual and team targets during a team meeting. The team leader is discussing the importance of meeting both individual and team targets.

"It's important that each of us meets our individual targets to contribute to our overall team success (individual frame). Remember, our collective effort is what drives our team's success (collective frame)."

Novelty vs. Tradition Framing

Novelty framing emphasizes new, innovative ideas or changes, while tradition framing underscores established practices or values. Leaders can use these frames to promote innovation, maintain continuity, or balance change with stability.

Example:

Context: A CEO is discussing a new but controversial initiative with senior executives during a board meeting. The CEO is trying to gain support for the new initiative.

"This initiative represents a bold and innovative step for us (novelty frame). But it's also a natural evolution of our longstanding commitment to customer satisfaction (tradition frame)."

CHAPTER 8: MOTIVATION

Following the same convention, I am beginning each chapter on the three skill sets by offering precise benchmarks so that you can evaluate your leadership and your team and pinpoint areas for improvement. I define Motivation this way. "Employee motivation is concerned with keeping people engaged and motivated by understanding their needs, values, and intrinsic motivators, and appealing to each person's particular worldview and leadership preferences."

Team Discussion

Use these questions when discussing this skill set with your team.

- How do we keep people engaged?

- How does our organization understand the needs, values, and motivators of individual team members?

- What are our current motivation methods?

- For each manager, how do you motivate your employees? What is your philosophy about motivating team members?

Benchmarks

Next we move into the benchmarks for this skill set.

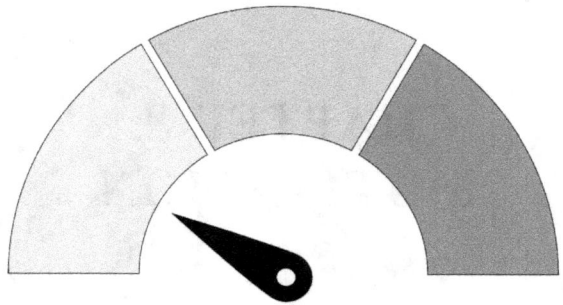

MOTIVATION LOWER RANGE

A leader and a team functioning in the lower range of proficiency in this skill set might describe it this way.

Some team members seem to be naturally motivated, and some seem to find our leadership style motivating, however, many members seem unmotivated by their work, the job and the team dynamics. Morale ebbs and flows and employee engagement is pretty low overall.

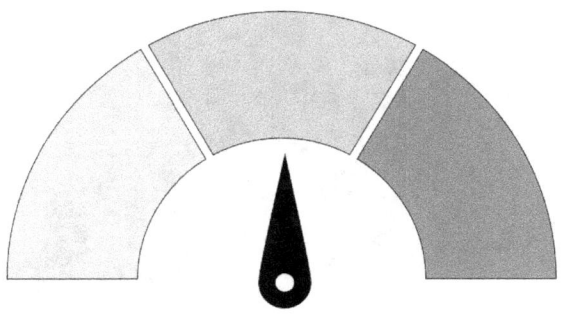

MOTIVATION MIDDLE RANGE

A leader and a team functioning in the middle range of proficiency in this skill set might describe it this way.

While we do make some efforts to motivate our people, I wouldn't say we are very good at it. We don't have tools or have the benefit of training on how to motivate people (such as using values, needs or styles to be more motivating). So while we have good intentions and put forth some effort, the level of motivation is pretty inconsistent.

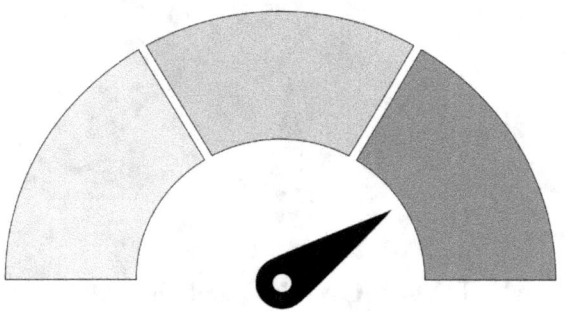

MOTIVATION HIGHER RANGE

A leader and a team functioning in the higher range of proficiency in this skill set might describe it this way.

We are serious students of leadership, including motivation. We are aware of our team members' needs and preferences, and are able to calibrate our messaging to them successfully so that most of the time it resonates with them and triggers their own intrinsic motivational drives. Our workforce overall is highly engaged.

Motivation Psychology for Leaders

Effective management is predicated on the ability to motivate people. This section offers many insights for leaders who want to become more effective at motivating their followers. As we will see in this section, <u>meaning is intrinsic to motivation</u>.

Most leaders have only a very rudimentary, and wholly inadequate grasp of the psychology of motivation. In particular, the Imperial Leadership Paradigm and the Traditional Leadership Paradigm (drawing inspiration from texts from the Bronze Age and Iron Age, and early Industrial Age) have a marginal grasp on motivation psychology. If you are serious about being successful in your leadership role, you really do need to understand how human motivation works. While you do not need to become an academic, you really do need to understand the basics of motivation theory. This section will provide that necessary foundation so that, going forward, you have a much better understanding about how human motivation works.

Many leaders are familiar with the pros and cons of extrinsic and intrinsic motivators popularized in management and leadership books, including Dan Pink's bestseller (and popular Ted Talk) *Drive*.

Extrinsic motivators are characterized by external, tangible, objective incentives and rewards, including pay and promotions. Intrinsic motivators are characterized by internal, intangible, and subjective factors such as autonomy, mastery, values, and purpose—in other words, meaning.

There is no such thing as an "unmotivated employee" or an "unmotivated workforce." Everyone is motivated, just in different ways and towards different activities.

Clearly, many workers are not motivated to do the things their leaders want them to do. But that doesn't mean they aren't motivated; they just aren't motivated to do the things they "should" be doing, according to their boss.

These same employees may be highly motivated to gossip with their coworkers, update their social media profiles, or finish the next level of an online game (rather than finish the report their manager is waiting for).

It's not that these employees are unmotivated; it's that they aren't motivated to do what you want them to do. And whose fault is that?

Who hired them?

Who on-boarded and trained them?

Who mentored and managed them?

Who is responsible for helping them understand what things mean in the organization?

As we are fond of saying, "leaders get the organizations they deserve."

If your employees aren't motivated to do the things you want them to do, then sharpening your knowledge and skills about motivation might be very beneficial.

Since everyone is motivated toward something, the key is to figure out what motivates specific people (or groups of people) in specific circumstances (or types of circumstances).

To support the goal of sharpening your understanding of motivation, and to simplify a complex and convoluted field, I will divide the hundreds of motivation theories into three distinct streams: 1. Instinctual Motivation Theories (biology-based). 2. Extrinsic Motivation Theories (goals-based). 3. Intrinsic Motivation Theories (values-based)

Instinctual Motivation Theories (Biology-based)

Clearly, the brain, biology, and instincts play an important role in human motivation. This theory was one of the earliest motivation theories proposed.

Over a hundred years ago, pioneering psychologist William James created a list of human instincts that included attachment, play, shame, anger, fear, shyness, modesty, and love.

And, instinctual theories are popular with contemporary evolutionary psychologists who emphasize the influence of genetic evolution on behavior.

Harvard Business School professors Paul Lawrence and Nitin Nohria claim that humans possess four fundamental instinctual motivators: to acquire, to bond, to learn, and to defend.

While the biology and brain amalgam represents an important piece of the motivational puzzle, it represents only one dimension of motivation.

Over time, in an effort to go beyond the many limits of the Instinctual Motivation Theories (biology-based), many researchers have focused on the influence of individuals' cognitive processes (e.g., beliefs about future events) and how those choices might lead to pain or pleasure.

Extrinsic Motivation Theories (Goals-based)

Extrinsic Motivation Theories focus on cognitive decision processes as an explanation of motivation.

These theories emphasize how individual behavior is directed and maintained specifically through self-directed cognitive processes—in simple terms, the carrot or the stick.

Some examples of these theories include Expectancy Theory, Goal-Setting Theory, and Reinforcement Theory.

Expectancy Theory looks at the factors associated with the degree to which workers believe that putting forth effort will lead to a given level of performance resulting in extrinsic outcomes or rewards, and how attractive those rewards are.

Goal-Setting Theory emphasizes the importance of specific and challenging goals in optimizing employee behavior.

Research supports that goals that are specific and challenging are more motivational than vague goals or goals that are too easy to achieve.

Reinforcement Theory posits that motivated behavior occurs as a result of reinforcers, which are outcomes resulting from the behavior that makes it more likely the behavior will occur again.

It also suggests that behavior that is reinforced is likely to continue, but behavior that is not rewarded (or behavior that is punished) is not likely to be repeated.

Extrinsic Motivation Theories such as these are based on the assumption that people are primarily motivated to pursue goals (external rewards) or avoid pain (external punishment).

Like the instinctual (biology-based) before them, these Extrinsic Theories do, in part, explain how some people are motivated, especially rational thinking, goal-oriented people who are focused on success (as measured by achievement).

Yet as business has more recently discovered, extrinsic motivation is both partial and limited.

In fact, recent research has shown that while extrinsic motivation methods can work well for certain types of algorithmic activities illustrated by tedious physical labor tasks, they can also significantly reduce motivation for more abstract activities that require creative solutions (the work "knowledge workers" do).

Intrinsic Motivation Theories (Values-based)

Intrinsic Motivation Theories are based on the assumption that people are motivated to engage in a given activity for its own sake because it is interesting and inherently valuable, as opposed to doing the activity to obtain an external goal.

We can start with a motivation theory that almost all readers are already familiar with and remains extremely useful today: *Maslow's Hierarchy of Needs.*

Some additional examples of intrinsic motivation theories include Clare Grave's *Emergent Cyclical levels of Existence Theory,* Cameron and Quinn's *Competing Values Framework* (popular in the corporate world), *Values and Lifestyles Inventory* or VALs (used extensively in the field of advertising and marketing), and Deci and Ryan's *Self-Determination Theory.*

Ryan's Self-Determination Theory was popularized by Dan Pink's book Drive and emphasizes the need and the value of feeling autonomous (self-determination) and having the opportunity to learn and grow.

McClelland's *Human Motivation Theory,* and much of the field of positive psychology, which is primarily concerned with human meaning, enjoyment, and engagement are also excellent intrinsic motivation frameworks.

In positive psychology, meaning is often described in terms of values and purpose. Values are what's most important (how people evaluate subjective experience), and purpose is the answer behind the question "why?"

One of the deepest and most meaningful questions a human can ask (and answer) is, "What is my purpose?"

The most fundamental and applicable aspects of meaning are, of course, values that play a central role in understanding intrinsic motivation.

Martin Seligman, one of the co-founders of the field, working with Christopher Peterson, developed the now-famous Values in Action Framework.

This values framework evolved into what positive psychologists call "virtues," which is another term for "universally held human values."

While all of these different frameworks can provide some value, especially for organizational psychologists, as leaders, we really need something a bit more simple.

The Second Simplicity of Intrinsic Motivation

The second simplicity of intrinsic motivation is the "The Twin Sisters of Intrinsic Motivation "

I can tell you after working with leaders and their organizations for more than 20 years, that in practical terms, in "organizational life," the two main things that motivate team members are needs and values, which are both intrinsic motivators. Yes, pay, bonuses and incentives (external motivators) do play a role, but a much smaller role than needs and values.

While the needs framework is very important to keep in mind, values (which are very closely correlated to the needs), provide even more utility for leaders wanting to understand and motivate their employees (or team members).

As a way to step into this topic in a meaningful way, I invite you to reflect on your context and your interest in motivating people. Please read and reflect on each the following questions one at a time. Do take a moment to really answer the question, at least in your head, ideally, writing down your answers. This will help bring this discussion out of the real of theory and concepts and into your specific context, where it matters most.

Why do you want to motivate people?

Who do you want to motivate?

What do you want to motivate them to do?

How do you currently motivate people?

Do you know how motivation works?

Have you considered the different ways people are motivated?

Now reflect on your leadership circumstances.

Who are the people that you want to motivate?

What specifically do you want to motivate them to do?

If it is convenient to do so, stop reading this book now and write down your list of people you want to motivate and write down specifically what you want them to do. This is important because these concepts aren't so valuable in a generic or textbook application, but they are extremely valuable if you relate them to specific people in your organization (or life) who you want to motivate!

If now is not a good time to stop doing this exercise, please make sure to do this activity later. Writing down their names and what you want to motivate them to do is an important step in this process.

Understanding People's Motivation

Consider two similar-sounding yet different questions.

- "How can I motivate this person?"
- "What motivates this person?"

At first glance, these questions seem to be asking the same question, but they are not at all the same question. Can you tell the difference?

The first question implies extrinsic motivation.

The second question implies intrinsic motivation.

In the case of the first question, "How can I motivate this person?", it implies extrinsic motivation.

You could offer the people something they want (for example; money or time off) ... or you could take something away from them that they want.

The second questions, "What motivates these people?" implies intrinsic motivations. It presumes they are already motivated.

The second question is another way to say "What is driving this person?" Or "What moves this person?" Or "What does this person care about?"

Extrinsic Motivation

Extrinsic motivation is also known as "carrot" and "stick" motivation. Rewards and punishment. Give them something they want or need or take away something they want or need. That is the carrot.

The idea here is to dangle something in front of them (like a carrot) to externally motivate them to move toward it.

Or introduce discomfort or pain, punish them in some way, and they will move away from that thing to avoid the pain or discomfort (the stick).

You already know how to do this. Parents often use this type of motivation for young children. And institutions often use this as well.

There are many examples of extrinsic motivation that begin with the letter "P." This can help you remember them. Pay, Privileges, Perks, Privileges, Penalties, Punishment.

Extrinsic motivation is inherently transactional in nature. Do this and get this privilege, pay or perk.

"Don't do that! If you do, you get _____" (penalty or punishment).

In a certain sense, it is a way to influence people from the outside. It forces people to comply to get what they want or need or to avoid receiving a penalty or punishment that they want to avoid. In truth, it is necessary, but it is also transactional (and it is often more effective than intrinsic motivation).

Intrinsic Motivation

Clearly, extrinsic motivation is not going away. It's quite necessary to use extrinsic motivation (incentives for compliance and consequences for non-compliance) to maintain order and/or control of large numbers of people, especially when the organization is larger than a reasonable number you can have a personal relationship with and therefore personal influence.

This section is about leadership not coercion. The difference between coercion (forcing people to do something) and leadership, is what we call "discretionary effort".

When a person "follows" someone whom they consider to be their "leader" then they are volunteering their faith in, belief in, emotional commitment to and "discretionary effort" to that leader. Therefore, leaders don't just coerce or manipulate people, they motivate and inspire people. And that is voluntary and comes from within (it is intrinsic).

Needs and Values

Needs are defined simply as "prerequisites for wellbeing and happiness." There are two kinds of needs or two "states" of needs.

Met needs and unmet needs. And we must differentiate them because needs in these two different states (met and unmet) have a very distinct and different psychological and emotional impact on humans, which includes your employees. Think of needs as a "threshold motivator." Until they are met, they are highly motivating. The need for security, the need for safety, the need for belonging, the need for respect, appreciate, fairness and so on. But once a need is met it disappears, or turns invisible and doesn't resurface in consciousness until it is unmet (drops below the threshold).

Unmet Needs - Unmet needs, or "unsatisfied needs" are highly motivating. Think how motivating it is when you feel hungry, thirsty, unsafe, unaccepted, unrecognized, unappreciated or feel that you are being treated unfairly.

Met Needs - Met needs, or "satisfied needs," are not motivating. They only exert a psychological influence when unmet. Once met, needs go into an invisible state. So met needs have little impact on motivation.

In terms of employee motivation, we focus on unmet needs. If an employee has unmet needs, then they have negative motivation, they are demotivated or motivated to resentment, bitterness, contempt or motivated to be looking for the soonest way they can find a better opportunity and leave. So in terms of employee engagement and motivation, we focus on any unmet needs that are creating reverse motivation, are demotivating, or worse causing unhappiness, resentment, bitterness, and so on.

Examples of unmet needs that you should address immediately to impact motivation and engagement include respect, appreciation and fairness. These are not the only needs that might not be being met, but these rise to the top of the list and are the ones you might want to scan for first.

Respect - Employees have a need for respect. If this need isn't being met, in other words if they feel disrespected, then addressing this, removing the factor that is causing it, or meeting their need for respect, is the first thing that should be done to improve engagement and motivation.

Appreciation - Employees have a need for appreciation, to feel appreciated. Employees need to know that their efforts matter and that their boss appreciates their effort. If this need isn't being met, in other words if they feel unappreciated, then addressing this, removing the factor that is causing it, or meeting their need for appreciation, is one of the first things that should be done to improve engagement and motivation.

Fairness - Employees have a need to be treated fairly. Another word for fairness is "equity." which is represented by the E in the very powerful and impactful (both good and bad) trend called DEI (Diversity, Equity, Inclusivity). Employees need to feel that they are being treated fairly or "equitably." If this need for fairness (equity) isn't being met, in other words if they feel they are being treated unfairly, then addressing this, removing the factor that is causing it, or meeting their need for fairness, is one of the first things that should be done to improve engagement and motivation.

Once an employee's basic "threshold needs" are met, they become invisible. Therefore, if an employee's basic needs are fulfilled, those needs are no longer a viable tool for motivation. At this point, we must turn to values.

Values are defined as "what is deemed most important" and "our highest priorities." Values are perceptual filters humans use to separate experiences and circumstances deemed "valuable" or good or desirable. Experiences (or circumstances) that do not meet our values or violate our values are deemed unwholesome, bad or undesirable (or in the case of traditional values, they are deemed "wrong" or "out of favor with an imagined higher power."

So, values are very very important and after the demotivating effect of "unmet needs," represent the most important factor in employee engagement and motivation. As many psychology experts have pointed out, it is not "pay, praise and perks" that are the chief motivators for employees. The primary motivation of all humans, including all employees, after unmet needs, is their values. And it should be obvious to any thoughtful reader that different people have different values (or value systems as they are called by psychologists, sociologists and market researchers).

If you want to know what motivates a person, you only need to understand their values. Their values are literally by definition "what is most important to them" or put another way, "What matters most to them." So a boss who doesn't know their employee's values is ignorant of what matters to that person and what that person cares about. Being ignorant of a person's values is to not know (or not care) about what that person cares about. As astonishingly obvious as this is, what is even more surprising is that a large percentage of leaders know little about values and value systems, and show little interest and put little effort into learning about and understand and appreciating their employees' values, or put another way, what a person cares about, what is important to a person and what matters to a person.

It is very difficult, next to impossible, to effectively motivate a person if your efforts are aligned with and centered around what that person cares about, what is important to that person, what matters to the person you want to motivate. In others words, how can you expect to motivate a person if you don't know (or don't care to know) what they care about?

By contrast, if you care enough to know what that person cares about, what matters to them, what is important to them—literally their values—then it is completely obvious what will motivate them, what matters to them and what they care about. Then you only need to "frame" your message, your assignments, your requests of that person in terms of their values (in terms of what they care about, what matters to them, what is important to them).

How to Know What Motivates a Person

Rather than ask how I can motivate this person? The better question for leaders is to ask, "What is motivating this person?"

That second question presumes that the person is already motivated.

It's another way to say, "What is driving this person?" or "What moves this person? Or "What does this person care about?"

As explained in this section, most people are being driven by or being motivated by unmet needs or values. If you know what to look and listen for, it is not difficult at all to recognize a person's unmet needs and values.

When we ask questions like, "What do they care about?", "What do they need?" "What matters to them?", and "What is important to them?" … we are essentially asking, "What do they need and what do they value?"

So, if there is a "leadership motivation shortcut" it is this.

First look for unmet needs. You must first plug those holes in your "employee motivation bucket" before doing anything else. Assuming the person doesn't have unmet needs such as a lack of respect, appreciation or fairness, then the next place to look is their values.

Find out what people value and you will KNOW what motivates them!

We are going to focus our limited time in this section on the topic of motivation on intrinsic motivation, specifically on understanding what already motivates people."

> *The crucial key to knowing how to motivate anyone is quite straightforward: you must pay attention and recognize what the person cares about. You must understand what they "value." And this is simply another way of saying, you must understand what is "important to them," what "matters most" to them or their "priorities."*

You must figure out why they would or should care about what you want them to do. Why would what you want them to do matter to them?

And you need to understand why they should do what you want them to do (in terms of what they care about, in terms of what they value).

Once you understand, then you simply "connect the dots" between what they care about and what you want them to do.

You must help them see why doing what you want them to do helps them achieve what they care about… is an expression of their deeply held values.

Values are the key.

If you are a leader who is serious about learning how to motivate people, then you must become a student of what motivates people.

Start paying attention to people's behaviors and ask yourself, "What is motivating this person?"

You may be surprised that it is fairly obvious once you start paying attention. It was right under our noses all along but it was invisible. It's easy to spot people's values if you simply take the time to look!

Think about the people in your personal and professional life. Reflect on what they care about.

What gets their attention? What do they find meaningful? What matters most to them? What do they place a high priority on? What do they value highly?

When you start asking these questions and pay close attention, especially if you have conversations with them and ask them questions about what they care about, you will quickly learn to spot people's values.

Examples of values:

Success

Achievement / Progress

Integrity

Personal growth

Fun

Honor

Duty

Honesty

Fairness

Safety

Security

Order

Respect

Loyalty

Responsibility

Professionalism

Advancement / Opportunity

Compassion

Relationships

What Do They Care About?

Take a moment to think about the different people and groups of people on whom you reflected on while reading the previous section.

Now select a person, team or group that you want to motivate.

If you can, write down the name of that person or group. At least bring this specific person or group to mind.

Now, ask yourself the following questions:

- What do they care about?

- What do they highly value?

- What do they say are their "values."

- What is most important to them?

- What seems to matter the most to them?

- What is driving their choices and behaviors?

- How do they describe their "beliefs," their "life philosophy" or their worldview?

Write down your answers to these questions or at least take a moment to reflect on them.

Now you need to answer the following question.

"Why should they care about what I want them to do, and why should they do what I want them to do?"

You need to figure out, according to what they care about, according to what they value, why they should care about the action you want them to take for their reasons.

You have to figure out why they should do what you are asking them to do for their reasons (according to their values).

Once you have figured that out, all you need to do is "connect the dots" for them so that they can see that doing the thing you are asking them to do is actually in their own interest and is an expression of their own values.

From this point forward, when you communicate to them about this, you frame the topic in terms of what they care about, their values.

This section has distinguished extrinsic motivation from intrinsic motivation.

We now can see that intrinsic motivation is crucial for leaders to use to help others recognize why they should care about what you want them to do for their reasons.

As you train yourself to recognize in others what they care about, what they value, you can begin to help them "connect the dots" between their values and what you are asking them to do.

As you begin to appreciate how values are held by others, you will gain additional insight into what is motivating some of the behavior and the choices of people you come across in your community.

Skillful leaders develop the ability to recognize other people's values accurately. This enables them to better understand a person's priorities and provides numerous clues about what decisions the person may make.

If you do not know what your employees value, then it is certainly going to be difficult to motivate them.

Have you asked them what is important to them about their role, their project, their assignment, and their teamwork?

Your employees are not motivated by your values, or necessarily the company's values, rather, they are motivated by their own values.

While some values have universal appeal (love, happiness, and health), most values cluster together based on a person's worldview and the environment in which they grew up and currently live and work.

To help you understand how the people in your organization to "make meaning," and what motivates them, I will now highlight four commonly seen "value clusters" that can also be thought of as meaning making or motivation clusters. This should come as no surprise to you that many values cluster together (according to worldview). When we look at values this way, we can see that there are four distinct ways that people are "driven" and you could say four different essential ways that people are motivated.

The Modern Worldview Values Cluster

Some people are motivated by success, achievement, and status. Surely you know people who fit this description.

They are concerned with personal autonomy, getting ahead, being at the top of their game, receiving recognition, living the good life, and especially winning.

You could say these are their priorities. These things are very important to them. They are motivated by these things.

These are their values.

People whose values fall primarily into this success and achievement cluster are likely to be more engaged in organizations and teams where the leader is perceived to have the most expertise and ability to achieve shared goals.

Think about it. If people are primarily or largely motivated by success and achievement, then they will appreciate and respect leaders who appear to have the knowledge, skills, and abilities to succeed in achieving the organization's shared goals.

We refer to this style of leadership as "Strategic Leadership".

It makes sense that men and women who highly value success and achievement would be very resonant with leaders who employ the "strategic leadership" style.

Modern Worldview - Motivation Reference Guide

Core Motivational Drivers - Achievement, success, status, opportunity, and winning.

Primary Concerns - Being "at the top of their game," achieving strategic goals, and personal autonomy.

Typical Goals and Desires - Getting ahead, living the good life, career advancement, receiving recognition, and again, winning.

In case it isn't totally obvious, the leadership technique here is to use your "framing" skill to frame your message in terms of the core drivers, primary concerns, goals and desires of the person you are attempting to influence.

The Postmodern Worldview Values Cluster

Some people are highly motivated by making a difference, harmonious interpersonal relationships, and personal growth.

People who are largely or primarily motivated by this cluster of values tend to be concerned with the quality of the connection in their relationships, cultivating self-awareness and peace of mind, fostering fairness and equality, and promoting human rights.

People whose values fall primarily into this cluster are likely to be more engaged in organizations and teams where the leader is perceived to be self-aware, who treats others as equals, who seeks out feedback and input, and who encourages discussion and consensus-building.

This style of leadership is called "Humanistic Leadership".

We refer to leaders who fit the above description as using the "Humanistic" leadership style. It makes sense then, that men and women who are motivated by this "Making a Difference" values cluster would be attracted to Humanistic leadership style, and would find this more credible, more trustworthy and more motivating based on their values and worldview.

Postmodern Worldview - Motivation Guide

*Core Motivational Driver*s - Diversity, equality, inclusion, personal growth and development, connection, and contribution

Primary Concerns - making a difference, cultivating harmonious relationships, spiritual growth, human rights, equality, inclusiveness and "ending systemic racism."

Typical Goals and Desires - Being self-aware, having peace of mind, building a diverse community, promoting equality, creating more diverse teams (and society), ensuring teams and organizations are "inclusive," and standing up for people who have less privilege.

In case it isn't totally obvious, the leadership technique here is to use your "framing" skill to frame your message in terms of the core drivers, primary concerns, goals and desires of the person you are attempting to influence.

Traditional Worldview Values Cluster

Some of the people in your organization are highly motivated by belonging, security, and preserving the traditional ways of thinking and acting according to how they were raised.

This group of values is called the "Traditional Values Cluster". People whose values fall primarily into this cluster are largely concerned with *fulfilling their duties, obeying authority,* and *doing the right thing* (as defined by their upbringing or the authority figures in their lives such as respected religious leaders).

As you would imagine, people who are primarily or largely motivated by these traditional values would gravitate toward leaders who are *seen as having positional authority and/or moral authority,* and who *loyally follow the established rules and the "chain of command"*.

Followers whose values fall primarily into this cluster are likely to be more engaged and motivated when their manager or leader is perceived to have positional and/or moral authority. The academic term for this authority-centric leadership is "Authoritarian" leadership, but we usually call it "Authority" leadership.

Followers with traditional values would be attracted to the Authority leadership style, and would find that style of leadership to be more motivating, more credible and more trustworthy than any of the other styles.

Traditional Worldview - Motivation Reference Guide

Core Motivational Drivers - Order, stability, security, self-sacrifice, and "Truth" (which for Traditionalists is almost always defined for them by their faith tradition).

Primary Concerns - Living according to "the one true way," fulfill one's duty, fitting in, preserving tradition, "doing the right thing. Again, for Traditionalists, what is "right" is always defined by the people they see as having positional or moral authority.

Typical Goals and Desires - Promote security and stability, faithfully following the rules and the dictates of their respected authorities, sacrifice now for future reward, defend Traditional beliefs and "natural laws," enforce rules and punish rule breakers.

Again, just reminding you that you combine these with your "framing" skill to frame your message in terms of the core drivers, primary concerns, goals and desires of the person you are attempting to influence.

Imperial Worldview Values Cluster

Some of the people in your organization are more motivated by *power, respect,* and *dominance.*

People whose values fall primarily into this cluster are often concerned with *being tough, gaining the upper hand, being able to protect themselves and their loved ones.* People motivated by this power-centric values cluster want to be *treated with respect.*

Followers who are motivated by this cluster of values would be attracted to the strong, tough, autocratic leadership style, and would find that style of leadership to be more motivating, more credible and more trustworthy (than some of the other styles we have discussed).

Followers with these values are likely to be more engaged in organizations and teams where the leader is perceived to be strong and dominant (or who is seen as capable of defeating their common enemies, we see this a lot with political leaders who appeal to people with this power values cluster).

As you recall, this style of leadership is described as "command and control" leadership or as it is widely recognized, "autocratic" leadership. It basically means that the one with the power, or who is perceived as being the most powerful, is the one who leads.

Imperial Worldview - Motivation Reference Guide

Core Motivational Drivers - Personal power, respect, freedom from constraint, uninhibited self-expression, asserting dominance.

Primary Concerns - Being "top dog", breaking free from limits, not being controlled by others, and gratifying desires.

Typical Goals and Desires - Gaining the upper hand, being in control, being seen as strong or tough, taking risks, breaking free from limits, being seen as the "alpha," and "going for the glory."

Again, you will use your "framing" skill to frame your message in terms of the core drivers, primary concerns, goals and desires of the person you are attempting to influence.

Conclusion

In this section, you learned about and how values motivate other people. We also took an initial look at values clusters and saw that people's values have a significant influence on the style of leadership they prefer to follow.

This concludes our discussion of the crucial motivation skill set. And with that, we round the corner to finish this deep dive "conversation" about how, as the subtitle of this book suggests, the most successful leaders create the container, communicate effectively, and consistently keep everyone engaged and motivated.

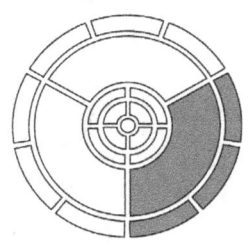

CONCLUSION: WHERE TO GO FROM HERE ON YOUR LEADERSHIP JOURNEY

Congratulations on completing this book. Research studies suggest that less than 50% of non-fiction book buyers actually finish the books they buy. Thank you for your determination to complete this one. Now that you have read this book, you have a strong familiarity with the fundamental leadership abilities and the nine leadership core competencies. You have also learned about numerous frameworks, tools and techniques that fall under each of the nine skill sets. While this is a very positive development, knowledge is not the same as skill. A skill is practice that has been engaged until it becomes a habit. If you want to improve your leadership, then must practice the techniques in this book. Developing the requisite skills described in this book will increase your competency in each of these dimensions. At minimum, you need to adopt and practice these techniques yourself. Experience shows that if you share some of these techniques with your team and invite them to practice these methods with you, as a team, you will learn them faster and your team will benefit from more than one person engaging in it.

Socializing these methods (techniques, behaviors) with your team will multiply the benefits for them.

As we learned in the section on "deliberate practice," practice doesn't make perfect, rather, perfect practice makes perfect. To increase your competency in these skill sets you have learned about, you must practice the techniques for many weeks (or months). This is the only way to learn a complex skill. You can't learn basketball from a book. You can't learn leadership from a book. But you can learn what you need to do in order to learn these techniques. We have used this method for 20 years helping leaders adopt new skills rapidly with consistent results. You can get the same results if you engage the practices described in this book.

I want to offer you a quick refresher about the principles of deliberate practice that are useful as implement this Integral Leadership methodology.

1) *Train technique* - To learn a complex skill, you must isolate the technique or skill, set specific goals based on best practices and benchmarks, practice with full attention and push beyond your comfort zone. You now know how to train.

2) *Rich feedback to calibrate and improve* - This involves practicing the techniques with full attention and effort, and obtaining immediate feedback to be able to calibrate and fine tune the new technique. One way to do this is to share the techniques and practices with your teammates so that they can give you feedback. The best feedback comes from people who have the skill. So if you have the opportunity to work with coaches or trainers who are familiar with these techniques, that will be ideal. This leads to the next key.

3) *You must get expert mentorship* – I have been able to provide an initial level of mentorship by describing these techniques. That is an excellent start, and if you are very disciplined and diligent in

practicing the methods as described, you can make some progress. However, mastery of these techniques, especially the more complex ones, requires getting individualized feedback and coaching from people who have legitimate expertise (who are experts in the specific techniques). Some of your coaches, advisors or trainers may be legitimate experts in one or more of these techniques (Creating the Container, Communication, Motivation). Take advantage of that.

Here's how to apply this knowledge to your situation:

1. Assess your current leadership approach – Identify your dominant leadership style and evaluate where you need to expand your versatility.
2. Develop your leadership skills deliberately – Focus on practicing specific leadership techniques using the deliberate practice framework outlined in this book.
3. Adapt to different followers and contexts – Use the Leadership Rosetta Stone to recognize the worldviews of those you lead and adjust your leadership approach accordingly.
4. Commit to ongoing growth – Leadership is not a one-time event; it is a continuous process of learning, refining, and improving.
5. Attend a course or coaching program where you can receive expert guidance and ongoing feedback to help you internalize the skills efficiently.

To increase your competency in these skill sets you have learned about, you must practice the techniques for many weeks (or months). This is the only way to learn a complex skill. To put this method into practice, active and ongoing training in the specific techniques is required. That is best done in a training and/or coaching environment. My partners and I, across numerous institutes and academies, offer numerous Integral Leadership training and coaching programs in various formats and at various price points to be able to accommodate most leaders in most circumstances. If you are serious about becoming a more effective leader, or if you support leaders (as a trainer or coach), I hope that you will pick up and read one or more of my other (longer, more detailed) books on this subject. You can find all of my books on Amazon.com. I also hope you will consider joining one of the many Integral Leadership training and coaching programs that my partners and I offer. My fourteen books are used as textbooks at multiple institutions and academies and offer various versions of my Integral Leadership training by several different names, including the Integral Leadership Program (many versions across several academies), the Integral Leadership MBA, the Executive Leadership Program and the C-Suite Leadership Program. When you participate in an in-depth online or in-person training based on this content, and especially if you obtain group or one-on-one coaching from a coach who has been trained in my content, then you will be able to rapidly accelerate your development as a leader, and ultimately become the kind of respected influential, impactful, successful leader you know that you are destined to be.

I look forward to continuing this "conversation" with you in one of my other books.

Brett Thomas

ABOUT THE AUTHOR

Leadership authority Brett Thomas is an expert on leadership development, integral theory, and developmental psychology. He has written 14 books on management and leadership. In collaboration with Ken Wilber, he created the world's first "unifying theory of leadership" and wove together 100 years of leadership theory into a unified model that explains which theories and approaches will work with which people and circumstances that also accurately predicts which leadership styles and approaches will be disastrous failures with which specific types of people and circumstances. He is the creator (along with his mentor Ken Wilber) of the popular practice known as Integral Leadership. Brett's fourteen books are used as textbooks around the world in many of the top leadership training and coaching programs. Numerous institutions and academies teach various versions of Brett's highly respected Integral Leadership Program, sometimes using other names such as the Executive Leadership Program, the C-Suite Leadership Program, and the Integral Leadership MBA. Brett is a serial entrepreneur and leader working behind the scenes in more than a dozen humanitarian efforts under the umbrella of the international non-profit (501c3) he quietly founded years ago. Brett is the mentor, advisor, and coach to hundreds of CEOs. Dozens of his clients have scaled their companies from tens of millions to hundreds of millions in revenue and even to over a billion in some cases (while going from dozens to hundreds to thousands of employees), always with a "balanced scorecard" and "triple bottom line," meaning a rich, healthy, beloved culture never merely profit-seeking. In addition to writing books, Brett serves as an advisor to dozens of CEOs and C-Suite Executive Teams, serves as a fractional COO to several organizations, and teaches in several academies. In addition to co-founding two of the most respected and admired leadership academies in the world, he is also one of the primary co-founders of the Conscious Capitalism movement, which he helped launch nearly two decades ago to make "business a force for good."

OTHER BOOKS BY BRETT THOMAS

Integral Leadership: The World's First Unifying Theory of Leadership That Will Forever Change How You Understand, Practice and Develop Leadership

Blowing the Whistle on Bogus Leadership: Veteran Industry Insider Reveals Why the Leadership Development Industry is Not Developing Leaders.

The Leadership Rosetta Stone: Discover Which Leadership Approaches Will Work With Which People and Circumstances and Which Approaches Will Be Disastrous Failures with Which People and Circumstances

The Universal Leadership Model: Simplicity on the Other Side of Complexity

Accelerating Leadership: The Groundbreaking Method for Rapid Leadership Skill Development That Achieves Twice the Results in Half the Time at a Fraction of the Cost

Reinventing Leadership: Discover the Revolutionary Method That Thousands of Leaders and Organizations Are Using to Rapidly Improve Leadership Performance and Organizational Results

Teamwork & Culture: How the Most Successful Leaders Create the Container, Communicate Effectively, and Consistently Keep Everyone Engaged and Motivated

Execution & Performance: How the Most Successful Leaders Close Expectation Gaps, Maintain High Accountability and Productivity, and Reliably Deliver Excellent Results
Worldviews: The Four Mindsets That Determine What People Perceive, Believe and Value, and Which Leadership Styles They Will Follow

Leadership Styles: How to Be a More Respected, More Influential and More Impactful Leader Using the Right Leadership Style With the Right People and Circumstances

Leadership Intelligence: Learn How Your Cognitive, Emotional, Social and Moral Development is Impacting Your Leadership Performance and How Leaders Can Now Benchmark and Boost These Intelligences

Measuring Leadership: How to Diagnose, Develop and Deliver Outstanding Leadership Performance by Benchmarking the Three Abilities and Nine Core Competencies That Matter Most (To be published in 2025)

Academic Books:

Handbook of Leadership Development: The Definitive Guide for Executives in Charge of Leadership Development

Leadership Psychology: How to Apply Crucial Insights from Positive Psychology, Developmental Psychology, Integral Psychology and Organizational Psychology to Develop More Effective Leaders (To be published in 2025)

www.ingramcontent.com/pod-product-compliance
Lightning Source LLC
Chambersburg PA
CBHW052143220526
45471CB00004B/1499